OBSERVATIONS

ON THE

LANGUAGE OF
CHAUCER'S HOUS OF FAME

AMS PRESS
NEW YORK

OBSERVATIONS

ON THE

LANGUAGE OF CHAUCER'S HOUS OF FAME

A DISSERTATION

Presented to the Faculty of the
University of Virginia for the Degree of
Doctor of Philosophy

BY

HARRY CLINTON FORD

Library of Congress Cataloging in Publication Data

Ford, Henry Clinton, 1867-1936.
   Observations on the language of Chaucer's Hous of fame.

   Reprint of the 1899 ed. printed by Stone Print. and Manufacturing Co., Roanoke, Va., which was originally presented as the author's thesis University of Virginia.
   1. Chaucer, Geoffrey, d. 1400. Hous of fame.
2. English language—Middle English (1100-1500)
I. Title.
PR1878.F6   1975   821'.1   76-168118
ISBN 0-404-02511-0

Reprinted from the edition of 1899, Roanoke
First AMS edition published in 1975
Manufactured in the United States of America

AMS PRESS INC.
NEW YORK, N. Y. 10003

INTRODUCTION.

THE following paper has as its first and chief aim to extend a little further the inquiry as to Chaucer's treatment of final *-e*. It is modelled closely on similar studies of the *Troilus* by Professor Kittredge, of Harvard, and of the *Legend of Good Women* by Professor Manly, of Chicago University, in the hope that the identity of form may add something to the value of them all.

In citing words from Old and Middle English in illustration of words and forms in the *Hous of Fame*, no attempt has been made to determine the dialect of Old English from which descent is to be traced, or to give a history of the changes which occurred between the Old English period and the time of Chaucer. The main object, as stated, has been to take some account of Chaucer's use of final *-e*.

The authorities for the *Hous of Fame* are few and very faulty. Almost any blunder might be attributed to the scribe who could perpetrate such monstrosities as *hytte* (= *hyt*), *whatte* (= *what*), *frerre* (= *fer*), etc. Numberless instances of wrongly written *-e*'s could be cited; and at the end of the verse no little difficulty has been had in deciding in certain cases whether or not the *-e* is of value. In general I have preferred to follow the guidance of Willert, who has taken quite a step forward in the suppression of these seemingly idle *-e*'s.

The present study is based on the Fairfax MS. 16, Bodleian Library, as being perhaps the best of the three; but careful comparison has been made with the other MSS., as well as with the editions of Caxton and Thynne. When the reading of another MS. than F is given, the fact is noted and the variants usually registered.

ABBREVIATIONS AND SIGNS.

A. R., Ancren Riwle, Morton, 1853; *B.*—*S.*, Bradley's Stratmann; *Freudenberger*, M. Freudenberger, Ueber das Fehlen des Auftakts in Chaucer's heroischem Verse, 1889; *He.*, Heath's edition of the poem in the Globe Chaucer; *L.*, Layamon's Brut, Madden, 1847; *M.*, Murray's New English Dictionary, Vol. I–II; *M. L. N.*, Modern Language Notes; *O.*, Ormulum, White, 1878; *O. & N.*, Owl and Nightingale, Stratmann, 1868; *P. Pl.*, Langland's Piers Plowman, Skeat, 1886; *Sheldon*, Sheldon's etymologies in Webster's International Dictionary; *Sk.*, Skeat's Etymological Dictionary and edition of the poem; *Sweet*, Sweet's History of English Sounds, 1888; *Wi.*, Willert's edition of the poem, 1888. Other contractions will be easily understood; such as *n.* (noun or neuter), *impv.* (imperative), *pp.* (perfect participle), etc. However, *adj.* means *adjective, singular, attributive*, unless *post.* or *pred.* is added; but when the adjective is invariable this distinction is not commonly made.

The following signs are used: -ë or -e = *e* pronounced; -e = *e* elided before a vowel or *h;* - ẹ = *e* apocopated or syncopated, as well when due to the scribe's caprice as in words in which it is regularly or sometimes sounded; (-e) = *e* unsounded in rhyme; [ ] indicates an omission in the MS.; ( ) marks something wrongly written within the verse; *f* (*as in* 2011 *f*) means *in rhyme;* ʽ marks the ictus; : expresses *rhymes with;* * denotes a line metrically imperfect which is not easily corrected by comparison of MSS.; ‖ marks the cæsura.

The manuscripts are denoted as follows: *F*, Fairfax MS. 16, Bodleian Library; *B*, Bodley MS. 638, Bodleian Library; *P*, Pepys MS. 2006, Magdalen College, Cambridge; *C*, Caxton's edition, British Museum, *about* 1483; *T*, Thynne's edition, 1532.

NOUNS.

§ 1. Masculine, feminine, and neuter nouns of the -*n* declension in Anglo-Saxon end in -*e* in *H. F.*

§ 2. I. Masculine nouns of the -*n* declension (Child, § 3).

Ape (A.S. apa, O. & N. ape), 1212 f (: iape *inf.*).

bane (A.S. bana, bona, L^a. bone, L^b. bane), 408 f (: Adriane *pr. n.*).

bere (A.S. bera), 1004 f (: here *pro.*).

grome (A.S. guma ; cf. O. N. gromr), 206.

hare (A.S. hara, O. & N. hare), 681 f (: fare *n.*).

make (A.S. gemaca, O. make), 1172 f (: make *inf.*).

mone (A.S. mōna, L. O. mone), 1531 f, 2116 f (*both* : sone *adv.*).

name (A.S. noma, nama, L. nome, name, O. name), 306 f, 558 f, 1145 f, 1275 f, 1312 f, 1411 f, 1462 f, 1489 f, 1556 f, 1610 f, 1620 f, 1696 f, 1716 f, 1736 f, 1761 f, 1871 f, 1900 f, 2112 f ; name, 346 ; name, 1877.

    Rhyme words. — shame *n.* (558), fame *n.* (the rest).

prikke (A.S. prica, pricca), 907 f (: thikke *pred. adj. sg.*).

shrewe (A.S. scrēawa, L. shrewe), 1843.

smoke (A.S. smoca, L. smoke), 769 f (: y-broke *pp.*) ; smoke, 1645 ; smoke, 743.

stere (A.S. stēora, *gubernator ;* stēor *n.*, O. ster, *gubernaculum*), 437.

sterre (A.S. steorra, L. steorre, sterre, O. steorne, P. Pl. sterre), 599 f (: ferre *comp. adv.*).

tene (A.S. tēona, L. teone, tuone, O. P. Pl. tene), 387.

tyme (A.S. tīma, L. O. time), 519 f, 1256 f (*both* : ryme *inf.*); tyme, 303, 1249 ; tyme, 536, 1257, 1523 ; tymes (*error for* tyme), 1155. — som tyme, 2088.

wele (A.S. wela, weola, L. wele, weole, P. Pl. weole), 1138 f (: fele *adj.*), 684 f (: stele *n.*).

welle (A.S. wella ; *but also* wielle, *m.*, wiell, *m.*, *and* wielle, *f ;* L^a. welle, wælle, L^b. welle, wel, O. wel), 522 f (: duelle 2 *pl. pr. ind.*), 1653 f (: helle *n.*).

wone (A.S. gewuna, L^a. iwune, wune, L^b. P. Pl. wone), 76 ; woone (*dwelling*), 1166 f (: to goone *ger. inf.*).

wrecch[e] (A.S. wrecc(e)a, wræcc(e)a, Sievers, § 89, n. 1. ; L^a. wræcche, wrehche, L^b. wrecche, wrech, O. wreche), 919.

§ 3. II. Feminine nouns of the -*n* declension (Child, § 4).

belle. (A.S. belle, L. O. belle), 1841 f (: telle *inf.*).

beme (A.S. bēme, bȳme), 1240.

chirche (A.S. cirice, cyrice, cyrce, L. circe, O. kirke, P. Pl. kirke, chirche), 473 f (: wirche *inf.*).

erthe (A.S. eorðe, L. O. eorðe, erþe), 752, 954, 1060, 1077, 1374 ; erthe, 715, 846, 918.

harpe (A.S. hearpe, L. harpe, hearpe), 773 f, 1201 f (*both* : sharpe *adv.*) ; harpe, 777 ; harp[e], 1005.

herte (A.S. heorte, L. heorte, O. heorrte, herrte), 373 f (: smerte *adj.*) ; hert[e], 315 f (: smert *adj. pl.*) ; 1799 f (: stert *3 sg. pt. ind.*) ; hert[e], 210, 326, 570, 1148, 1814 ; herte, 604, 1749. Except in our MS. *-e* is commonly written.

larke (A.S. lāwerce, P. Pl. larke), 546 f (: starke *adj. def. post. pl.*).

pipe (A.S. pipe, O. & N. pipe), 1219 f (: pipe *inf.*) ; pipe, 773, 774.

Rose (A.S. rōse ; *also* O. F. rose), 135.

sonne (A.S. sunne, L^a. sunne, L^b. sonne, O. sunne), 497.

syde (A.S. sīde, L. O. side), 1419 f (: wide *adj. pl.*) ; syde, 1204 ; syde, 1151.

tonge (A.S. tunge, L O. tunge), 348 f, 721 f, 1234 f, 1656 f ; tong[e], 2022 f.

> Rhyme words. — songe *pp.* (348, 721), yonge *adj. pl.* (1234), y-ronge *pp.* (1656), y-sprong *pp.* (2082).

wyse (A.S. wīse, L. O. wise), 1061 f, 1114 f (*both* : deuyse *inf.*), 1347 f (: venyse *pr. n.*).

§ 4. III. Neuters of the -*n* declension (Child, § 2).

ere (A.S. ēare, O, ǣre), 2044 f, 2058 f (*both* : there *adv.*).

yë (A.S. ēage, L. eʒe, O. eʒhe), 291 f, 498 f, 906 f, 935 f, 1492 f.

> Rhyme words. — lye *n.* (291), hye *adv.* (498, 906), Galoxie *n.* (935), hye *adj.* (1492).

§ 5. In *lady* (A.S. hlǣfdige, *f.*) the final vowel disappears.

lady (A.S. hlǣfdige, L^a. læfdi, læudi, lafdie, L^b. lafdi, O. laffdiʒ), *before consonants*, 204, 213, 1311, 1536, 1593, 1609, 1677, 1693, 1704, 1730 ; *before vowel*, 1310.

§ 6. Anglo-Saxon masculine and neuter vowel-stems that have a final vowel (*-e* or *-u*) in the nominative singular, preserve this vowel as *-e* in *H. F.* (cf. Child, § 7).

For convenience the following classes of nouns are thrown together in a single alphabetical list : (i.) masculine *jo-*(*ja-*)

stems with long stem-syllable, — *ende;* (ii.) neuter *jo-(ja-)* stems with long stem-syllable, — *stele;* (iii.) masculine *i*-stems with short stem-syllable, — *hete, lyge, stede;* (iv.) neuter *i*-stems with short stem-syllable, — *spere;* (v.) masculine *u*-stems with short stem-syllable, — *sunu.* Masculine nomina agentis in *-ere* (which properly belong under i.) and abstract nouns in *-scipe* (which properly belong under ii.) lose *-e;* see § 7.

ende (A.S. ende, *m.*, L. O. ende), 1646 f, 1867 f, (*both:* wende *inf*.

-ere, see § 7.

hat*e* (A.S. hete, *m.* (cf. hatian), L. hæte, hete, L^b. hate, O. hete, hate), 95, 1964.

lye (A.S. lyge, *m.*), 292 f (: ye *n.*), 1552 f (: companye *n.*).

sone (A.S. sunu, *m.*, L. sune, sone, O. sune), 218 ; son*e*, 138 165, 177. — son*e*, 160 ; sonne, 941.

> Note. — Ten Brink's remark — "*sone, wone* kommen im Vers nie als zweisilbig vor" (*Spr. u. V.*, 261) — is contradicted by verse 218 : *Syth that he hir sone was.*

spere (A.S. spere, *n.*, L. spere, sper, P. Pl. spere, sper), 1048 f (: were *1 pl. pt. ind.*).

stede (A.S. stede, *m.*, L. stude, O. stede, O. & N. stede, stude), 829 f (: drede *n.*) ; stid*e*, *827. — stede, 731.

stele (A.S. stēle, style, L. stel), 683 f (: wele *n.*). But Willert prefers to conform the rhyme–word to the ordinary usage of *stele*, as is seen by his writing *steel, weel.* Skeat and Heath, on the other hand, retain *-e.* — stel(e), 1130 f (: euerydele).

§ 7. Exceptions to § 6.

The termination *shippe* (A. S. -scipe, *m.*, *jo*-stem) occurs but once, and *-e* is unsounded. A. S. -ere, *m.*, *jo*-stem, is seen in but one word ; in this *-e* is dropped.

stele, see § 6.

-ere (A.S. -ere, *also* L. W. S. -re, *m.* ; Sievers, § 248) : harper Orion, 1205.

-shippe (A. S. scipe, L^a. -scipe, L^b. -sipe): frendshìppe, 307.

§ 8. Anglo-Saxon feminine vowel-stems that have *-u* in the nominative end in *H. F.* in *-e* throughout the singular (except in the genitive).

The following list includes (i.) *ā-(ō-)* stems with short stem-syllable : *faru, lufu, sagu, sceadu, scealu, sceamu, talu;* (ii.) abstract nouns in *-u, -o*, corresponding to Gothic abstracts in *ei* and usually indeclinable in the singular: *brǣdu*, *hǣlu*, *hǣtu;* (iii.) feminine consonant-stem with short stem-syllable: *hnutu*.

brede (A.S. brǣdu, Lᵃ. brǣde, Lᵇ. brede, O. & N. brede), 1494 f (: rede *1 sg. pr. ind.*); bred*e*, 2042.

fare (A.S. faru, L. fare, fære, uore, P. Pl. fare), 682 f (: hare *n.*), 1065 f (: clare *pr. n.*).

hel*e* (A.S. hǣlu; *also* hæl, -e, *f.*, L. hele, O. hæle), 1966.

hete (A.S. hǣtu; *also* hæte, -an, *f.*; L. hate, O. hæte), 569 f (: bete *inf.*), 921 f (: wete *pred. adj.*), 940 f (: strete *n.*), 1149 f (: bete *n.*); hete, 1164.

loue (A.S. lufu; *also* lufe, -an, *f.*, see Sievers, § 279, n. 1, Cosijn, *Altws. Gr.* II, §§ 33 and 14, Platt, *Anglia*, VI, 176; Lᵃ. lufe, Lᵇ. loue, O, lufe, P. Pl., love), 321, 1235, 1797, 2143; love, 1757 f (: above *adv.*); lou*e*, 243, 247, 258, 305, 625, 634, 683, 1056, 1711, 1739, 1995; lov*e*, 277, 1889, 1964. — louẹ, 341, 1697, 1758.

> Note. — Four examples of final sounded -*e* within the verse are recorded; of these there can be no question as to but one:
> Ther men of louë tydynges tolde; *or, possibly,*
> Ther men of louẹ tydynges tolde, 2143.

note (A.S. hnutu; cf. O. N. hnot; P. Pl. wal-note), walsh note, 1281.

sawe (A.S. sagu, L. saȝe, sæȝe, P. Pl. sawe), 2089 (: thrawe *inf.*).

shade (A.S. sceadu; *also* scead *n.*, see Sievers, §§ 260, 271), 1160 f (: made *3 sg. pt. ind.*).

shale (A.S. scealu, scalu, Lᵃ. scale, Lᵇ. scole, P. Pl. scale, shale), 1281 f (: tale *n.*).

shame (A.S. sceamu, scamu, sceomu, Lᵃ. scome, sceome, scame, Lᵇ. same, seame, O. shame), 557 f (: name *n.*), 1582 f, (: diffame *inf.*), 1816 f (: fame *n.*); sham*e*, 1655.

tale (A.S. talu, L. O. tale), 1282 f (: shale *n.*), 1839 f (: pale *n.*); tal*e*, 1829.

§ 9. Monosyllabic feminine nouns with long stem-syllable take in *H. F.* a final -*e* (perhaps derived from the oblique cases) throughout the singular, except in the genitive (cf. Child, § 16; ten Brink, § 207).

The following list includes: (i.) *ā*-stems, — *bǣr, bōt, healf, heall, hēord, lār, lēaf, mīl, rest, rōd, sāwol, scond, spǣc, stefn, stund, strǣt, hevīl, wund;* (ii.) *jā*-stems, — *bliðs, hell, hȳr, -nis;* (iii.) *wā*-stems, — *lǣs, mǣd, rǣw;* (iv.) *i*-stems, — *bēn* (influenced by O. N. *bōn*), *dǣd, flōr, hȳf, gecynd, gemynd, nīed, cwēn, cweorn, gesihð, tīd;* (v.) consonant-stem, — *mūs;* (vi.) *hēahðu, on lengðe,* O. N. *slǣgð, slǣwð, strengðu, trēowð, untrēowð.* For convenience *derthe* and *routhe* are included in this section.

bere (A.S. bǣr, bēr, L. O. bære), 1744 f, (: chere *n.*).
blysse (A.S. blīðs, bliss, L. O. blisse), 492 f (: wisse *inf.*).
— blys, 2016 f (: amys *adv.*).
bone (O. N. bōn, bœn, *f.*, A.S. bēn, O. bene, L. bone), 1537 f, 1774 f (*both* : sone *adv.*).
bote (A.S. bōt, L. O. bote), 32.
dede (A.S. dǣd, dēd, L. dede, O. dede, dǣd-bote), 329 f (: godelyhede *n.*), 386 f (: rede *inf.*).
derthe (A.S. dēore, *adj.* ; cf. O. N. dȳrð ; P. Pl. derthe), 1974.
flore (A.S. flōr ; also *masc.*, Sievers, § 274, n. 1 ; L. flor, O. flor), 1344, 2033.
halfe (A.S. healf), 1136. For *half, adj.*, cf. 1345 ; *adv.*, 914, 1923.
halle (A.S. heall, hall, L. halle), 1314 f, 1527 f, 1533 f, 1568 f, 2142 f ; halle, 1357, 1514, 1826 ; halle, 1186, 1342, 1493.
> Rhyme words. — alle *pro.* (1314), with alle (1527, 2142), falle *inf.* (1533), calle *inf.* (1568).

helle (A.S. hell, L. helle, O. helle), 445 f, 1510 f, 1654 f, 1803 f ; helle, 441 ; helle, 72, 918.
> Rhyme words. — telle *inf.* (445, 1510, 1803), welle *n.* (1654).

herde (A.S. hēord, L.ᵃ. heorde, L.ᵇ. hierde), 1225.
hight[e] (A.S. hēahðu, hēhðu, hīehðu), 740 f (: wight *pondus*), 744 f (: lyght *adj. post. plur.*). But -e nowhere appears in either *hight* or the rhyme-words.
hire (A.S. hȳr, L. hure, P. Pl. hure, huire, huyre), 1857 f (: a fire).
hive (A.S. hȳf), 1522 f (blyve *adv.*).
kynde (A.S. cynd, *n.*, gecynd, *f.*, (later *n.*) ; late A. S. gecynde, *n.*, and gecyndu, -o, *f.*, Sievers, § 267 b. and n. 4 ; L. icunde, cunde, O. kinde), 43 f, 584 f, 749 f, 824 f, 1213 f.
> Rhyme words. — fynde *3 pl. pr. ind.* (43), mynde *n.* (584, 824), fynde *1 sg. pr. ind.* (749), behynde *prep.* (1213).

lengthe (A.S. on lengðe ; *also* lengu, -o, *f.*), 1979 f (: strengthe *n.*) ; lengthe, 1370 ; length (+ *vowel*), 1494.
lese (A.S. lǣs), 1768 f (: ese *n.*).
leve (A.S. lēaf, L.ᵃ. leue, lǣue, leaue, lefe, leaf, L.ᵇ. leue, lefue, O. lefe), 2105 f (: eve *n.*) ; leve, 1089.
lore (A.S. lār, L.ᵃ. lǣre, lare, leore, L.ᵇ. lore, O. lare), 579, 1965.
mede (A.S. mǣd, mēd ; *gen.*, mǣdwe, mǣde ; L. medewe, *dat.*), 1353 f (: rede *inf.*).

muse (A.S. mūs, P. Pl. mus), 785 f (: house *n.*). All authorities show *-e* here, and Wi., Sk. and He. retain it. It is quite probable, however, that we here have to do with one of the numberless idle *-e*'s. The uniform usage of the rhyme word elsewhere strengthens this notion.

myle (A.S. mīl, L. O. mile), 1038.

mynde (A.S. gemynd, *f.* and *n.*, O. minde), 583 f, 823 f (*both :* kynde *n.*) ; mynde, 564.

nede (A.S. nīed (also *n.*, cf. Cosijn, *Altws. Gr.* II, § 26), nēd, nēad, nēod, L. ned, neod, neode, O. ned, *acc.* nede), 724 f (: drede *n.*), 1011 f (: spede *3 sg. pr. subj.*); nede, 1342, 2137.

-nesse, *termination*, (A.S. -nes, -nis, -nys, L. O. P. Pl. -nesse), feblenesse, 24. — godenesse, 1854 f ; godenes, 1832 f. — heuynesse, 2011 f. — lyknesse, 1080 f. — sekenesse, 25 f ; sekenesse, 1966.— shrewdenesse, 1627 f, 1853 f.— wikkednesse, 1813 f ; wikkednes, 1831 f. — worthynesse, 1628 f.

> Rhyme words. — Nouns in *-nesse* except the following : distresse *n.* (25, 2011), gesse *inf.* (1080, 1813).

quene (A.S. cwēn, cwǣn ; also cwēne, -an, cf. Cosijn, *Altws. Gr.* II, § 26 ; L^a. quen, quene, L^b. cwean, cweane, cwene, O. cwen), 1409 f (: sustene *inf.*), 1535 f (: shene *voc. post. adj.*) ; quene, 241, 1512. — quene, 1271.

querne (A.S. cweorn, cwyrn), 1798 f (: werne *inf.*).

reste (A.S. rest, ræst, L^a. reste, *dat.*, L^b. raste, *dat.*, O. resste), 2017 f (: breste *inf.*) ; reste, 654 ; rest (+ *vowel*), 1956.

Roode (A.S. rōd, L. O. rode), 2 f, 57 f (*both :* to goode *prep. phr.*).

routhe (not in A.S. ; formed from the verb *reouwen*, A.S. *hrēowan*, on the analogy of other abstract nouns in *-th* ; cf. O. N. hrygð, hryggva ; L^a. reoðe, reouðe, L^b. rouþe), 332 f, 383 f, 396 f, 614 f ; routhe, 2012.

> Rhyme words. — trouthe *n.* (332, 614). vntrouthe *n.* (383, 396).

rowe (A.S. rāw, rǣw, A. R. a rewe, P. Pl^c. rewe, by rewe), 448 f, 1451 f, 1835 f ; rewe, 1692 f.

> Rhyme words. — knowe *inf.* (448, 1451), fewe *pro.* (1692), knowe *pp.* (1835).

shonde (A.S. sceond, scond, sceand, scand, L. sconde, O. shande), 88 f (: stonde *inf.*).

sleight (O. N. slœgð, slægð ; not in A.S. ; L^b. slehþe, *dat.*, sleahþe, *nom.*, sleþþe, P. Pl^b. sleighte, P. Pl^c. sleithe), 462 (+ *vowel*).

slouthe (A.S. slǣwð, L. slauðe, P. Pl^a. sleu3the, P. Pl^b. sleuthe), 1764 f (: trouthe *n.*).
soule (A.S. sāwol, L. saule, O. sawle), 1612 ; soul*e*, 43.
speche (A.S. sprǣc, sprēc, L. W. S. spǣc, spēc, L. spǣche, speche, O. spǣche), 781 f, 1071 f, 2066 f ; spech*e*, 278, 331, 783, 818, 824, 832, 849, 856, 1028 ; spech (+ *vowel*), 762, 1074. There is but a single example before a consonant (766). Here PCT, correctly, —
And euery spechë that is spoken ; F B, —
And euery spech that ys yspoken.
    Rhyme words. — teche *inf.* (781, 1071), eche *inf.* (2066.).
stevene (A.S. stefn, stemn, L. stef(e)ne, steuene, O. steffne), 561 f (: nevene *inf.*).
stound*e* (A.S. stund, L. stunde, O. stunnd), 2071.
strengthe (A.S. strengðu, strengð, L. strengþe, strenðe, O. strennc þe), 1980 f (: lengthe *n.*).
strete (A.S. strǣt, strēt, L^a. strǣte, stret, L^b. strǣt, O. strǣte), 939 f (: hete *calor*), 1049 f (: fete *n.*).
syghte (A.S. gesihð, L^a. siht, *nom.*, sehte, isihðe, sih3eðe, *dat.*, L^b. seht, *nom.*, sihte, *dat.*, O. sihhþe), 468 f (: highte *3 pl. pt. ind.*) ; syght[e], 1016 f (: bryght *adv.*). But in the latter example all omit -*e* in both *syght* and the rhyme-word.
trouthe (A.S. trēowð, trēowðu, L. treouðe, O. trowwþe), 331 f, 613 f, 1763 f ; trouthe, 297, 889 ; trouth*e*, 807.
    Rhyme words. — routhe *n.* (331, 613), slouthe *n.* (1763).
tyde (A.S. tīd, L. tide, *dat.*, O. tid), 1951 f (: wide *pred. adj. pl.*).
vntrouthe (A.S. untrēowð), 384 f, 395 f (*both* : routhe *n.*).
while (A.S. hwīl, L. while, O. whil, while), 415 f (: Ile *n.*), 1287 f (: berile *n.*), 1484 f (: Virgile) ; while, 1417 ; whilë hee, 904 ; whil*e*, 1019, 1994.
wounde (A.S. wund, L. O. wunde, *obl.*), 374.

§ 10. Nouns in *-yng*, *-ynge*.
I. There is in *H. F.* no case of a noun in *-ynge* rhyming with an infinitive.
II. Here follow all cases in rhyme of nouns (including "gerunds") in *-ynge*. Where no note is added, the rhyme-word is another noun in *-ynge*.
askynge, 1700 f (: thinge *n.*). — blodeshedynge(s), 1241 f. — clarionynge(s), 1242 f. — enclynynge, 734, f (: thynge *n.*). — fleynge, 1523 f. — forswerynge, 153 f. — humblynge, 1039 f. — knowynge, 892 f (: thinge *n.*). — lesynge, 154 f. — murmuryng, 1524 f. — sterynge, 800 f (: goynge *pres. part.*). — thundringe, 1040 f.

12

III. Nouns in *-yng*, *-ynge*, before consonants.
comynge, 537. — crowdyng, 1359. — felynge, 552.— gynnynge, 66. — kunnynge, 1168, 2056. — weddynge, 244. — writynge, 1161.

IV. Nouns in *-yng*, *-ynge*, before vowels.
axyng, 1541. — betynge, 1034. — engendrynge, 968. — holdynge, 692.— lesynge, 2089.—magnyfyinge, 306. — movynge, 812. — rowtynge, 1933. — turnynge, 182. — wepinge, 1199. — wynnynge, 1972.

§ 11. The following feminine nouns with long stem-syllables do not take *-e* in *H.F.* (cf. Child, § 17) :

(i.) *ā*-stems, — *feoht;* (ii.) *i*-stems, — *miht, þrift, wiht, weorold;* (iii.) consonant-stems, — *bōc, niht*.

For other feminine nouns which in *H. F.* sometimes or always lack final *-e*, cf. *loue*, § 8 ; *blys, -nesse, quene*, § 9 ; nouns in *-ynge*, § 10 ; and *hond*(e), § 13.

boke (A.S. bōc, L. O. boc), 1093 ; booke, 429 ; boke, 712 ; booke, 426 ; at another book(e), 656 f (: looke *n. nom.*).

fyght (A.S. feoht, fyht, L. feht, fæht, feiht, feoht, fiht, *dat.* fihte, fuhte), 1241 (+ *vowel*). This example is of course not decisive.

myght (A.S. mi(e)ht, meaht, L. mihte, O. mihht, mihhte), 41 f, 49 f, 80 f, 528 f, 1091 f, 1693 f, 2023 f, 2146 f ; myght (*vowel*), 971.

Rhyme words. — a-nyght (41), aryght (49, 80, 528, 2023), lyght *n.* (1091), bryght *post. adj. voc.* (1693), wight *n.* (2146).

nyght (A.S. ni(e)ht, neht, neaht ; L. niht, O. nihht), 112 (+ *cons.*) ; a-nyght, 42 f (: myght *n.*) ; a nyghte, 632 ; be nyght (+ *vowel*), 1953.

thrift (O.N. þrift), 1847 (+ *cons.*) ; thrifte, 1786.

wight (A.S. wiht, wuht, wyht, *f.* and *n.*, Sievers, § 267, n. 3 ; L. wiht, whit, O. wihht, P. Pl[b]. wyght, P. Pl[c]. wight, wiht, wiȝt), 1076 f, 2061 f, 2145 f ; wyght, 1830 f ; wight(e), 1626 f ; *before consonants*, wight, 1808, 2043 ; wyght, 276, 1565 ; *before h*, wight, 1682, 1877.

Rhyme words. — ryght *adv.* (1076, 2061), lyghte *post. adj. sg.* (1626), a ryght (1830), myght *n.* (2145).

world (A.S. woruld, W. S. weorold ; L. weorld, weorlde, weoreld, weoruld, woreld, world, worlde, O. weorelld), 1932 (+ *cons.*) ; world hyt, 1525 ; worlde, 100, 1640, 1721, 1746, 2038 ; worlde, 906, 1674, 1770, 1807. In 1724 we have a harsh verse, but it can hardly be that we should read *worldë* :
That through the worlde went[e] *the soun*.

§ 12. Apocope of A.S. -*n* in nouns is found in *H. F.* in the following words (cf. Child, § 15 ; ten Brink, §§ 203, 207).

eve (A.S. æfen, ēfen, *n*. and *m*., L^a. æuen, L^b. heue, O. efenn), 876 f (: leve *1 sg. pr. subj.*), 2106 f (: leve *n.*).

game (A.S. gamen, gomen, *n.*, L. gomen, gamen, game), 664 f, 822 f, 886 f, 1199 f, 1474 f; game, 1810.

  Rhyme words.— Fame *n.* (664, 822, 1199, 1474), Iame *pr. n.* (886).

morwe (A.S. morgen, margen, *m*., L. morʒen, morʒe, morwe, P. Pl. morwe, morwen), morwë how, 225 ; morwë or, 2106.

wyndmelle (A.S. wind + mylen, *m*.), 1280 f (: telle *inf.*).

§ 13. *Hand* (A.S. hond, *fem. u-stem.*).

honde (A.S. hond, hand, *f.*, L. hond, hand, *dat.* hande, honde, O. hand, wiþþ hand, hande), on honde, 1009 f (: stonde *3 pl. pr. ind.*) ; in honde, 1877 f (: stonde *1 sg. pr. ind.*) ; in hys honde, 171 f (: of the londe) ; with your ryght honde, 322 f (: bonde *n. nom.*) ; on my ryght hond(e), 1294 f (: fonde *1 sg. pt. ind.*) ; hand*e* hit, 741.

  It will be observed that final -*e* is written in all the examples cited. Moreover, this -*e* uniformly appears in all other authorities save 171 (BPC). Certainly it is sounded in the phrases *on honde, in honde,* (1009, 1877), — the rhyme words evidence that. But it is clearly wrong when rhyming with *fonde, 1 sg. pt. ind.* (1294). Is it not probable then that -*e* is equally idle in 171, 322? Note the rhyme words. Wi., Sk. and He., however, all retain -*e*.

§ 14. The following masculine and neuter nouns which in Anglo-Saxon end in a consonant in the nominative, sometimes or always take an -*e* in one or more cases in *H. F.* :

(i.) masculine *o*-stems,— *circul, clūd, epistol, fǣr (fēr), -hād, hēap, heofon, hræfn, mūð, pīn, slǣp, weg;* (ii.) neuter *o*-stems, — *bond, cræt, fȳr, gæt (geat), gēar (gēr), gōd, hūs, līf, lond, scip, swefen (swefn), tempel, wolcen;* (iii.) neuter *i*-stems, — *gefēr, (ge)wiht;* (iv.) masculine consonant-stem, — *fot*.

The MSS. of the *Hous of Fame* are very imperfect, and in almost numberless cases final -*e* is written uniformly when it manifestly has no value. Scansion is a nearly infallible test of this when the word occurs within the verse, and at the end the rhyme-word frequently settles the matter with certainty. Disregarding then the cases in which -*e* can thus be proved idle, these words seem to have final -*e* mainly in certain " petrified phrases " (cf. Kluge in Paul's *Grundriss*, I, 900). These are the phrases which have led to the belief that the regular ending of the dative in Chaucer is *-e*, whereas, as a matter of fact, the dative occurs much more commonly without *-e* than with it. It is in these idiomatic phrases that *-e* is sounded, — phrases which had probably come to be accepted and written without analysis and without conscious inflection (compare the modern acceptance of such expressions as *afire, alive, asleep*). The dative ending was preserved in these idioms, but the force of the dative as such was no longer felt (cf. Kittredge and Manly, § 14). This is pretty certainly the explanation of final *-e* in the following phrases found in *H. F.* : *for fere, a fire, a lyve, on lyve, on slepe, to yere.* To these we may add with reasonable certainty *to goode, on an hepe*, and perhaps *to shippe*. With these we should include *in fere*, unless we take it that *gefēr* has been influenced by *gefēra*.

But no such explanation accounts for *fote* in *half a fote, a fote brede of space* ; and the same remark holds for *mouthe, pyne*, both of which follow prepositions. In the case of *bonde, -hede, house, londe*, there is at least reasonable doubt whether *-e* should be pronounced. In *cercle* (A.S. circul) and *temple* (A.S. tempel) the *-e* is compensatory for the loss of an interior vowel. Compare also *heuene* (A.S. heofon), *sweuene* (A.S. swefen), *wolkene* (A.S. wolcen), in which it is hard to say whether the ultimate or the penultimate *-e* is sounded. For many examples of idle final *-e* in masculine and neuter nouns, see § 18, below.

bonde (A.S. band, *n.* (bande, *pl., Pet. Chron.*), Sweet, 254 ; but the regular A.S. form is *bend, m.* and *f.*, see Sievers, § 266, n. 2 ; O. band), *nom.*, 321 f (: with your ryght honde). But is *-e* sounded here ? It is uniformly written, and Sk. and He. retain it. See, however, observation under *honde*, § 13.

borde, see § 18.

carte (A.S. cræt, *n.*, L. carte, O. karrte, P. Pl. cart-whel), Hym slowe and fer from the cart cast[e], 956. But PCT are more likely correct : Hym slowe and fro the cart[ë] cast[e]. — carte, *nom.*, 944 ; carte, *acc.*, 943.

cercle (A.S. circul, *m.*, but influenced by O. F. *cercle*), *nom.*, 815 ; sercle, *nom.*, 791 ; a litel roundell as a sercle, 791 f (: couercle *n.*).

cloude (A.S. clūd, *m.*, L. clude), *acc.*, 978.

deth, see § 18.

epistile (A.S. epistol, pistol, *m.*), *acc.*, 379.

fere (A.S. gefēr, *n.*, perhaps influenced by gefēra, *m.*, or even confused with it ; L^a. ifere, iueore), in fere, 250 f (: manere *n.*).

fere (A.S. fǣr, fēr, *m.*), for fere, 604, 1042 ; in al hys fere, 174 f (: were *3 pl. pt. ind.*) ; fer*e*, *acc.*, 607.
fire (A.S. fȳr, *n.*, L. fur, *dat.* fure, O. fir), a fire, 1858 f (: hire *n.*) ; fir*e*, *nom.*, 2078 ; be fir*e*, 742 ; of fir*e*, *1976.
fote (A.S. fōt, *m.*, L. fot, *dat.* fote, O. fot, o fot, wiþþ fote), half a foote, 1345 ; A fote brede of space, 2042. — barefote, 98.
goode (A.S. gōd, *n.*, O. god, inn gode, forr gode), to goode, 1 f, 58 f (*both* : Roode *n.*) ; good(e), *acc.*, 1714 f (: woode *pred. adj. pl.*), 1748 f (: for wode *madly*). — good*e*, *acc.*, 1088 ; good (+ *cons.*), *acc.*, 1566, 1998 ; good (+ *vowel*), 1628, 1795, 1975.
grounde, see § 18.
-hede (suffix, A.S. hād, *m.*, L^b. child-hode, man-ede ; O. maȝȝdenn-had, maȝȝþ-had ; P. Pl. maiden-hod, man-hede, man-hod, knyght-hod), godelyhede, 330 f (: dede *n.*) ; godelyhed(e), 273 f (: hede *n. acc.*). It is quite certain that -*e* is not pronounced in the latter example, and the same may be true of the first.
hepe (A.S. hēap, *m.*, L. hæp, hep, *dat.* -e), on an hepe, 2148 f (: lepe *inf.*).
heuene (A S. heofon, *m.*, also L. W. S. heofone, *f.*, Bright, s. v., L. heouene, heofne, O. heoffne, heffne), in heuene, 1008 f, 1254 f ; heuene, *acc.*, 1375 f ; *before consonants*, (dissyllabic), to the heuene, 164 ; to heuene, 591 ; of heuen, 1087 ; *before vowels*, to the heuen*e*, 495 ; be-twexen heuen*e*, 715 ; in heuen, 949 ; amyddys . . . . heuën, 846.

> Rhyme words. — sevene (1008, 1375), nevene *inf.* (1254).

hors, see § 18.
house (A.S. hūs, *n.*, O. hus), to Fames house, 786 f (: of a Mouse). In this example the several authorities are a unit in showing -*e*, and Wi., Sk. and He. retain it. It seems quite probable, however, that this -*e* should not be sounded. — in al that hous that, 1064 ; this hous hath, 1945 ; vpon this hous tho, 1989 ; in this hous was, 2030 ; hous (+ *vowel*), 891, 1070, 1105, 1114, 1925, 1935, 1977, 1987, 2121 ; hous*e* 484, 655, 663, 821, 882, 1023 ; hous*e*, *nom.*, 1942 ; hous*e*, *acc.*, 1920 ; in fames hous*e*, 1027.
londe (A.S. land, lond, *n.*, L. lond, *dat.* londe, O. land, P.Pl^a. lond, P.Pl^b. *dat.* londe), of the londe, 172 f (: in hys honde) ; withouten . . . lond(e), 485 f (: [of] sonde) ; ouer al thys lond*e*, 348. But -*e* can hardly be sounded in the second example in rhyme, and it is doubtful if it should be in the first ; see remarks under *honde*, § 13, above.

lyve (A.S. līf, *n.*, L. lif, on liue, bi life, bi liue, O. lif, *dat.* lif, life), on lyve, 1168 f, a lyve, 2055 f.

Rhyme word. — descrive (discryve) *inf.*

lyf(e) *acc.*, 176 f, 423 f, 457 f; lyf*e*, *nom.*, 36; lyf*e*, *acc.*, 258; lyfe, *acc.*, 1414; *phrases*, al thy lyf(e) (*acc. of time*), 200 f; of lyf(e), 1963 f. In the foregoing examples FBT regularly show final -*e*, while PC lack it. Wi., Sk. and He. omit -*e* except in 1963. The justification for this distinction is not apparent.

Rhyme words. — wife *n.* (176, 200, 423, 457), stryfe *n.* (1963).

mouthe (A.S. mūð, O. muþ, A.R. muð, O. & N. muþ), Out of his trumpes mouthe smelde, 1685; Of euery Philosophres mouthe, 757 f (: kouthe *adv.*); to hys mouth(e) (B P C mouth), 1679 f (: southe *adv.*); fro mouthe to mouth(e) (B C mouth), 2076 f (: southe *adv.*). It can hardly be that -*e* is sounded in the last two examples.

pyne (A.S. pīn, *m.* (?), L. O. pine), with ful moche pyne, 147 f (: Labyne *pr. n.*); of the derke pyne, 1512 f (: Proserpyne *pr. n.*); with al[le] pyne he, 222.

Raven*e* (A.S. hræfn, hræm, *m.*), *acc.*, 1004.

shippe (A.S. scip, *n.*, L. scip, schip, *dat.* schipe, P.Pl. ship, schup), to shippe, 420.

slepe (A.S. slǣp, *m.*, L^a. on slæpe, L^b. a-slepe, O. slæp, o slæpe), on slepe, 114; the god of slep*e*, 69; to slep*e*, 112.

sothe, see § 18.

swevene (A.S. swefen, swefn, *n.*, L^a. sweven, swoven, *dat.* swefne, L^b. sweven, *dat.* swevene, P.Pl^a. swevene), 9 f (: ev*e*ne *adv.*); sweuen*e*, *acc.*, 79.

temple (A.S. tempel *n.*), 469, 1858; templ*e*, 1844.

tovn*e*, see § 18.

welkene (A.S. wolcen, wolcn, *n.*, *pl.* wolcnu, *Pet. Chron.* se wolcne, L. weolcne, wolcne, P.Pl^b. walkene, welkne, P.Pl^c. wolkene), in alle the welken*e* (*or* welk*e*ne), 1601.

weye (A.S. weg, *m.*, L^a. wæi, wai, wei, weie, L^b. wai way; *dat.* L^a. waie, waiȝe, etc., L^b. weie, waye, O. weȝȝe), of the wey[e], 714 f (: sey *inf.*); but C alone shows -*e*. — wey(e), *acc.*, 937 f (: parfeye); all the wey, 969; be no way, 1258; goo your wey, 1622, 1561 f (: welaway); a forlong*e* way, 2064.

wife, see § 18.

wight[e] (A.S. gewiht, *n.*, also gewihte, *n.* (Sweet, 896), L^a. wiht, L^b. weht, O. wehhte), 739 f (: hight *n.*); but the several authorities lack -*e* uniformly.

yate (A.S. gæt, W. S. geat, *n.*, L. ȝæt, ȝet, ȝæte, ȝate, O. ȝate), *acc.*, 1294.

yere (A.S. gēar, gǣr, gēr, *n.*, L. ȝer, *dat.* ȝere, O. ȝer), to yere, 84 f (: here *3 pl. pr. subj.*). — euery yere, 302.

§ 15. The following nouns (chiefly Germanic), for which no corresponding Anglo-Saxon etymons can be cited, sometimes or always end in H. F. in -*e* :

(A.) Suspicious or uncertified Anglo-Saxon words, — *mone* (A.S. *mān, inferred from *mǣnan*), wenche (A.S. *wencel, *pl.* winclo). (B.) Words from Old Norse, — *lathe, lofte, sherte, skye, trust, tydynge, wyndowe*. (C.) Probable Middle-English formations from Anglo-Saxon words, — *bete, clappe, drede, ferde, hede, swappe, wente*. (D.) Of doubtful etymology, — *gonne, were*.

bete (A.S. bēatan, *vb.*), with stormes bete, 1150 f (: hete *n.*).

clappe (A.S. clappan, *vb.* ; cf. M.Du. klap, O.H.G. chlaph), 1040.

drede (A.S. drǣdan, *vb.*, L. dred, drede, P.Pl. dre(e)de), 31 f, 551 f, 723 f, 830 f, 1142 f, 1456 f, 1913 f ; drede, 1971. — drede, 292.

> Rhyme words. — bede *inf.* (31), dede *inf.* (551), nede *adv.* (723), stede *n.* (830), rede *inf.* (1142, 1456), lede *inf.* (1913).

ferde (A.S. fǣran, *vb.* ; cf. M. H. G. ge-vǣrde, *f.*, *n.*, ' betrug '), for ferde, 950.

gonne (Celtic ? cf. Sheldon, s.v. *gun*), 1643 f (: ronne *pp.*).

hede (cf. O.Fris. hûde, hôde, O.H.G. huota, *f.* ; P.Pl^b. hede), 787.

lathe (O.N. hlaða, *f.*), 2140 f (: rathe *adv.*).

lofte (A.S. on lofte (Napier, *M.L.N.*, V, 278, Kluge, Paul's *Grundriss*, I, 786 ; from O. Norw., O. Icel. loft, *n.*, later Icel. lopt), on lofte, 1726 f (: softe *adv.*).

moone (A.S. *mān, cf. mǣnan, *vb.* ; P.Pl^c. mone), 362 f (: to done *ger. inf.*).

shert[e] (A.S. scyrte, *f.* ; from O.N. skyrta, *f.* ; L. scurte, P.Pl^c. sherte), That with a shert[e] hys lyfe les, 1414.

skye (O.N. skȳ, *n.*), 1600 f (: hye *adv.*).

swappe (A.S. *swāp, cf. swāpan, *vb.*), in a swappe, 543.

trust (O.N. traust, *n.*), 1971 (+ *vowel*).

tydynge (cf. O.N. tiðindi, *m.*, L. tidinge), for oo tydȳnge, 2109 f (: wringe *inf.*). — tydynge, 648, 2045, 2072, 2111, 2134 ; tydynge, 2066.

wenche (A.S. *wencel, *pl.* winclo, O. wenchel, P.Pl^a. wenche), 206 f (: drenche *inf.*).

went [e] (A.S. wend, *f.* ?), 182 f (: went *3 pl. pt. ind.*).
were (Scotch weir, cf. Skeat, *Minor Poems, Glossary*), in a were, 979 f (: here *adv.*).
wyndowe (O.N. vindauga, *n.*, P.Pl. windowe), At a wyndowë yn me broughte, 2029. But CT are probably correct : And at a wyndow*e* yn me broughte. — wyndow*e*, 2084 ; wyndow*ẹ*, 2091.

§ 16. The following monosyllables may be put together : sǣ (*i*-stem *m., f.*), strēaw (*wo*-stem, *m.*), trēo(w) (*wo*-stem, *n.*), wā (*intj.*).

see (A.S. sǣ, partly *m.*, partly f., cf. Sievers, § 266, n. 3 ; L. sæ, se, O. sæ), 133 f, 255 f, 715 f, 748 f, 751 f, 846 f, 903 f, 1034 f ; se, 417 f ; see, 238, 923, 1361, 1984.
  Rhyme words. — partee (133), shee *pro.* (255), three *adj.* (715, 846), see *inf.* (748), bee *3 pl. pr. ind.* (751), hee *pro.* (903, 1034), be *inf.* (417).
stre (A.S. strēaw, strāw-berie, strēa(w)berie, North strē, Rush. strēu, Sievers, §§ 112, n. 1 and 3, 250 n. 1 ; P.Pl^{bc}. strawe), 363 f (: he *pro.*).
tree (A.S. trēo(w), *n.*, North trē, trēo, trēu(o), Sievers, § 250, 2 ; L. treo, O. treo, tre), 484 f (: see *inf.*), 1108 f (: see *1 sg. pr. subj.*).
woo (A.S. wā, *intj.*, cf. wea, *wk. m.*, L. wa, O. wa, waȝȝ), what me ys woo, 300 f (: two) ; a woo and routhe, 396.

§ 17. In the following nouns final -*y* comes from the vocalization of an Anglo-Saxon -*g*. Cf. also *wey* (§ 14), *lady* (§ 5).
body (A.S. bodig, n.), 981, 1063, 1081, 1230 (*slur*), 1759.
day (A.S. dæg, *m.*), 111 f (: lay *1 sg. pt. ind.*), 227 f (: array *n.*), 1284 f (: say *vidi*) ; day, 63, 1157, 1951.

§ 18. The following masculine and neuter nouns, which in Anglo-Saxon end in a consonant in the nominative, take no -*e* in *H.F.* even in the dative.

(i.) Masculine *o*-stems,[1] (*a*) monosyllabic, *brǣð, catt* (?), *ceap, cinn, cleric, cniht, copp, cræft, cwealm, cyning, dēað, dōm, drēam, fisc, flod* (*m., n.*), *gāst, ge-þoht, god, grund, heals, hearm, hām, hōd, horn, hring, hrōf, lust, stān, strēam, taegl, top*(*p*), *tūn, weall, wind ;* (*b*) dissyllabic, *castel, dēofol,* (*m., n.*), *eornest, fugol, hlāford, þunor, tācen ;* (ii.) neuter *o*-stems,

---

[1] *U*-stems that have in Anglo-Saxon completely identified themselves with the *o*-declension are not here distinguished from *o*-stems.

—(*a*) monosyllabic, *bæc, blōd, bord, bræs, brēost, būr, corn, fers, folc, ge-sceap, glæs, gold, græs, hǣr, hors, hwēol, īs, lēac, lēad, leoht, los, mist, rīm, scinn, sond, sōð,* þ*ing, weorc, wīf, wit*(*t*)*, word ;* (*b*) dissyllabic, *brægen, furlong, hēafod, iren, tæppet, timber, wæter, wundor ;* (iii.) masculine *jo-*stem, — *pyt*(*t*) *;* (iv.) masculine *i-*stems, — *dǣl, dynt, gest, hyll ;* (v.) neuter *i-*stem, — *flǣsc ;* (vi.) masculine *u-*stems, — *feld, sumor ;* (vii.) masculine consonant-stems, — *frēond, monn* (and compounds) ; (viii.) neuter consonant-stem, — *cild.*

NOTE. — In the above list are included : (1) nouns which show no *-e ;* (2) nouns in which a final *-e* is elided before vowel or *h*, and which have not been observed in the *Troilus* or *L. G. W.* with sounded *-e ;* (3) nouns in which final *-e* is manifestly unsounded ; (4) a few nouns at the end of the verse, in some of which it is barely possible that *-e* should be pronounced, — *corn, hēafod, hōd, horn, lēac, sond, tūn, weal*(*l*)*, word.*

bak(e) (A.S. bæc, *n.*), behynde hys bak(e), 977 f ; at my bak(e), 1869 f ; on hys bakk*e*, 169.

Rhyme word. — spake *1 and 3 sg. pt. ind.*

blood(e) (A.S. blōd, *n.*), *acc.*, 201 f (: woode *pred. adj. sg.*), with tigres blod*e*, 1459.
bonde, see § 14.
borde (A.S. bord, *n.*), ouer bord*e*, 438.
bour(e) (A.S. būr, *n.*), *nom.*, 1186 f (: toure *n.*).
bras (A.S. bræs, *n.*), table of bras, 142 f ; trumpe of bras, 1637 f.

Rhyme word. — was *3 sg pt. ind.*

brayn (A.S. brægen, *n.*), of my brayn, 525 ; of her brayn(e), 24 f (: sayne *3 pl. pr. ind.*).
brest (A.S. brēost, *n.*), in my brest, 1109.
breth (A.S. brǣð, *m.*), *nom.*, 1684.
castel (A.S. castel, *m.*), 1162, 1176, 1185, 1196, 1294, 1917, 1919.
catt(e) (A.S. catt, *m.*), lyke the swynt[e] catt(e), 1783 f (: whatte *pro.*).
chep*e* (A.S. cēap, *m.*), of chep*e*, 1974.
child (A.S. cild, *n.*), *nom.*, 920.
chyn (A.S. cin, *m.*), in . . . . chyn, 1230 f (: skyn *n.*).
clerk (A.S. cleric, clerc, *m.*), *nom.*, 1487.
cop (A.S. copp, *m.*), vpon the cop, 1166.
corn(e) (A.S. corn, *n.*), of grene corn(e), 1224 f (: horne *n. nom.*). C alone, however, lacks *-e*. Wi. has *corn ;* Sk. and He. retain *-e*.

crafte (A.S. cræft, *m.*), *nom.*, 1213 ; *acc.*, 1100.
del (A.S. dǣl, *m.*), euerydel, *acc.*, 880 f ; dele, *acc.*, 331 ; euerydel(e), *nom.*, 1129 f ; *acc.*, 65 f ; be a thousande del(e), 1495 f.
    Rhyme words. — wel *adv.* (880, 1495), wele *adv.* (65), stele *n.* (1129).
deth (A.S. dēað, *m.*), *nom.*, 323, 502 ; dethe, *acc.*, 404 ; of my deth, 325 ; fro the dethe, 413 ; of deeth, 1963.
deuel (A.S. dēofol, *m., n.*), The deuel be hys soules bane, 408 ; fouler than the deuel, 1638.
dom(e) (A.S. dōm, *m.*), of her dom(e), 1905 f (: come *1 sg. pt. ind.*).
dreme (A.S. drēam, *m.*), *nom.*, 9, 50 ; *acc.*, 1, 58 ; dreme, *acc.*, 62, 517, 527 ; of my dreme, 511 ; in dreme, 917.
dynt (A.S. dynt, *m.*), *nom.*, 534.
englissh (A.S. englisc, *adj.*), *acc.*, 510.
ernest (A.S. eornest, -ost, *m., f.*), in ernest, 822.
felde (A.S. feld, *m.*), *nom.*, 486 ; feld(e), *acc.*, 482 f ; in the Feld(e), 540 f.
    Rhyme word. — behelde *1 and 3 sg. pt. ind.*
fyssh (A.S. fisc, *m.*), *nom.*, 751 ; fissh, *acc.*, 1784 ; fisshe, *acc.*, 1003.
flesh (A.S. flǣsc, *n.*), *nom.*, 49.
floode (A.S. flōd, *m., n.*), *nom.*, 72 ; in floode, 751.
folke, see § 43.
forlonge (A.S. furlong, furlang, *n.*), a forlonge way, 2064.
foule (A.S. fugol, *m.*), *nom.*, 539.
frende (A.S. frēond, *m.*), *voc.*, 1871, 1873 ; frende, *nom.*, 582.
gest (A.S. gæst, gest, giest, gyst, gist, *m.*), *acc.*, 288 f (: lest *n.*).
glas (A.S. glæs, *n.*), *nom.*, 1289 f ; of glas, 120 f, 1124 f.
    Rhyme word. — was *pt. sg. ind.*
God (A.S. god, *m., n.*), *nom.*, 1 ; god, *nom.*, 74 ; vnto the god of slepe, 69 ; to this god, 77.
gold (A.S. gold, *n.*), *nom.*, 1387 ; golde, *nom.*, 272 ; with gold, 1386 ; of gold, 1346 ; of golde, 122, 1765 ; of golde, 503, 1678 ; of gold(e), 530 f (: tolde *pp.*).
gost (A.S. gāst, *m.*), in gost, 981 f (: wost *2 sg. pr. ind.*) ; gost(e), *nom.*, 185 f (: oste *n.*).
grass (A.S. græs, W.S. gærs, *n.*), withouten . . . . grass, 485.
greke (A.S. Grēc, Crēc), throgh the greke Synon, 152.
grounde (A.S. grund, *m.*), fro the grounde, 905.
hals (A.S. heals, *m.*), ryght be the hals, 393 f (: fals *pred. adj. sg.*).

harme (A.S. hearm, *m.*), *nom.*, 99, 383 ; *acc.*, 265, 577, 1566 ; harme, *acc.*, 1045, 1677.
hede (A.S. hēafod, *n.*), *acc.*, 632, 1021 ; hed(e), *acc.*, 136 f (: rede *adj. sg. def. post.*) ; hed(e), *acc.*, 273 f (: godelyhede *n.*) ; hed(e), *acc.*, 1702 f (: dede *pred. adj. pl.*) ; in thy hede, 621 ; by my hed(e), 1875 f (: dede *adj. sg. pred.*) ; in myn hede, 1103 ; with her hed she, 1375. —— in my heued, 550 f (: a-sweued *pp.*).
heere (A.S. hǣr, hēr, *n.*), *nom.*, 1386.
hille (A.S. hyll, *m.*), of this hille, 1152 ; vp the hille, 1166.
hod(e) (A.S. hōd, *m.*), in her hod(e), 1810 f (: wode *pred. adj. pl.*). All authorities show -*e*, however, and Sk. and He. retain it ; not so Wi.
home (A.S. hām, *m.*), thou goost home, 655.
horn(e) (A.S. horn, *m.*), *nom.*, 1223 f (: of grene corne). All authorities have -*e*, which Sk. and He. retain ; Wi., however, drops it.
hors (A.S. hors, *n.*), made the hors broght, 155.
house, see § 14.
knyghte (A.S. cniht, *m.*), *nom.*, 226.
kynge (A.S. cyning, cyng, *m.*), *nom.*, 159, 515, 916 ; kynge, *nom.*, 105, 1789 ; with kynge, 453 ; by heuen kyng(e), 1084 f (: thynge *n.*).
lede (A.S. lēad, *n.*), *nom.*, 739 ; of lede, 1431, 1445 ; lede, *nom.*, 1448 ; led(e), *acc.*, 1648 f (: rede *pred. adj. sg.*).
lek(e) (A.S. lēac, *n.*), *acc.*, 1708 f (: eke *adv.*). But -*e* is uniformly written by all authorities.
les (? A.S. lēas, *adj.*), withouten les, 1464 f (: Achilles).
londe, see § 14.
lord (A.S. hlāford, *m.*), *voc.*, 1395 ; lorde, *voc.*, 1393 ; lorde, *nom.*, 206 ; lord(e), 258 f (: at oo worde). In the last example all save C show -*e*, but Wi., Sk. and He. all omit it.
losse (A.S. los(s), *n.*), For ese of you and losse of tyme, 1256.
luste (A.S. lust, *m.*), *acc.*, 258.
    lest (cf. A.S. lystan), be . . . her nyce lest, 287 f (: gest *n.*).
lyght (A.S. leoht, *n.*), of lyght, 1091 f (: myght *n.*).
man (A.S. monn, mann, *m.*), 10, 32, 60, 99 f, 144 f, etc., etc.
mouthe, see § 14.
myst(e) (A.S. mist, *m.*), 352 f (: wiste *pp. sg.*).
pitte (A.S. pyt(t), *n.*), *nom.*, 1654.
qwalme (A.S. cwealm, cwalm, *m.*), of qwalme, 1968.
roof (A.S. hrōf, *m.*), *nom.*, 1344 ; on the rove, 1948.
ryme (A.S. rīm, *n.*), *nom.*, 1096 ; in Ryme, 623.
ryng(e) (A.S. hring, *m.*), *nom.*, 1740 f (: thynge *n.*).

shap (A.S. gesceap, *n.*), *acc.*, 1113.
skyn (A.S. scinn, *n.*, A.S. Chr. 1075 ; from O.N. skinn), *acc.*, 1230 f (: chyn *n.*).
slepe, see § 14.
sonde (A.S. sand, sond, *n.*), [of] sonde, 486 f (: londe *n.*). But the several authorities show -*e* uniformly.
somer (A.S. sumor, *m.*), in somer, 1947.
soth*e* (A.S. sōð, *n.*), *nom.*, 351 ; sooth, *acc.*, 1552 (+ *vowel*) ; soth*e*, *acc.*, 2108 ; *acc. in phrases*, soth for to, 563, 1368 ; soth*e* for to, 563, 960 ; soth to, 1842 ; soth*e* to, 1388, 1804, 1917 ; the soth*e* to, 1509 ; *other phrases*, of . . . sooth (+ *cons.*), 1029 ; in sooth (+ *cons.*), 1057. —— But, — for sothë, *adv.*, 1873.
sterisman (A.S. stēormann, *m.*), *acc.*, 436 f (: began *3 sg. pt. ind.*).
ston, stoon (A.S. stān, *m.*), *nom.*, 656 f, 739, 1123, 1605 f ; *acc.*, 790 f ; of ston (stoon), 70 f, 1184, 1584 f ; of the ston, 1933 f ; vpon a stoon, 1991 f.
> Rhyme words. — anoon *adv.* (70, 656, 790, 1605), gon (goon) *inf.* (1584, 1933, 1991).

strem*e* (A.S. strēam, *m.*), vpon a strem*e*, 71.
tayll*e* (A.S. tægl, tægel, *m.*), *acc.*, 880.
thing (A.S. þing, *n.*), *nom.*, (+ *vowel*), 1367, 2147 ; *nom.*, thyng*e*, 730 ; euery thing*e*, 753, 835 ; any thing*e*, 738 ; thyng*e*, 739, 746, 781, 1292 ; euery thing*e*, 351, 828 ; thyng(e), 733 f, 1083 f ; *acc.*, thing (+ *cons.*), 1020, 1650, 1774 ; thing (+ *vowel*), 2002 ; thing*e*, 587, 1279 ; thing*e*, 1068, 2060 ; euery thing*e*, 1291 ; thing(e), 891 f ; of thing that, 959 ; of thys thyng to, 239 ; of thys thyng*e*, 53 ; with somme maner thing*e*, 670 ; lyke a thyng*e*, 1124 ; for no maner other thing(e), 1699 f. —— no thing*e*, *nom.*, 350, 1044 ; *acc.*, no thing nolde, 1780 ; nothyng*e*, 575 ; no-thing*e*, 425 ; *adv'l*, no thyng*e*, 1346 ; no thing*e*, 2032.
> Rhyme words. — enclynyng*e n.* (734), knowyng*e n.* (891), kyng*e n.* (1083), askyng*e n.* (1699).

thonder (A.S. þunor, *m.*), of thonder, 534 f, 608 f ; lowde as any thunder, 1681 f.
> Rhyme word. — wonder *n.*

thought (A.S. geþoht, *m.*), *nom.*, 1923 f ; *acc.*, 1174 f ; *voc.*, 523 ; in her thoght, 92 f ; in thoght, 329 ; of thought, 973.
> Rhyme words. — y-wrought *pp.* (1174, 1924), noghte *adv.* (92).

tipet (A.S. tæppet, *n.*), on thy tipet, 1841.

token (A.S. tācen, tācn, *n.*), *acc.*, 911 f (: spoken *pp.*). F B P lack the verse.
toppe· (A.S. top(p), *m.*), *acc.*, 880.
toun (A.S. tūn, *m.*), *acc.*, 484 f (: Region *n.*) ; in euery toun, 1580 f (: clarioun *n.*) ; withouten . . . tovne, 484 ; tovn(e), *acc.*, 890 f (: adovne *adv.*) ; in the tovn(e), 1849 f (: of grete renovne).
tymber (A.S. timber, *n.*), *nom.*, 1980.
vers (A.S. fers, *n.* ; cf. O.F. vers), *nom.*, 1098.
walle (A.S. weal(l), *m.*), on a walle, 141 ; wall(e) (F *alone* -e), *nom.*, 1343 f (: alle *omnia*) ; on the wall(e) (F *alone* -e), 211 f (: with-alle). There seems no real ground for the distinction made by Wi., Sk. and He. in retaining -*e* in 211 and omitting it in 1343, particularly when the variants in both cases uniformly lack -*e*.
water (A.S. wæter, *n.*), on water, 789 ; of the watir, 814.
werke (A.S. weorc, *n.*), of olde(*l.* golde) werke, 127 ; of good werke(s), 1558.
wif(e) (A.S. wif, *n.*), *nom.*, 175 f ; to hys wif(e), 424 f, 458 f.
    Rhyme word. — lyfe *n. acc.*
wit (A.S. wit(t), *n.*), *nom.*, 1180 ; *acc.*, wit, 1898 f ; wyt, 950 f, 1175 ; wytte, 16 ; wytt(e), 328 f, 620 f ; of wit, 1972 ; to my witt(e), 702 f, 1377 f ; to my wytte, 3.
    Rhyme words. — yit *adv.* (328, 950, 1898), yitte *adv.* (620, 1377), hytte *pro.* (702).
wynde (A.S. wind, *m.*), *acc.*, 1598 ; wynde, *nom.*, 1803 ; with wynde, 230 ; the god of wynd(e), 1571 f (: blynde, *pred. adj. sg.*). But the passage in which the last example occurs is corrupt. CT show *wynde* rhyming with *fynde inf.*, and Sk. and He. adopt this reading ; not so Wi.
whele (A.S. hwēol, *n.*), *nom.*, *794 ; *acc.*, 1450 ; whel(e), *acc.*, 794 f (: wel *adv.*).
woman (A.S. wīfmann, *m.*), *nom.*, 261, 269, 279, 1082.
wonder (A.S. wundor, *n.*), *nom.*, 913 ; *acc.*, 533 f, 607 f, 1069 f, 1378, 1682 f ; wounder, *acc.*, 806 f.
    Rhyme words. — thonder (thunder) *n.* (533, 607, 1682), vnder *adv.* (806), yonder *adv.* (1069).
word (A.S. word, *n.*), *nom.*, 881 ; *acc.*, 1080 ; with this word, 884, 960 ; of euery word, 877 ; worde, *nom.*, 809 ; *acc.*, 819, 1077 ; with this worde, 2027 ; with that worde, 1567 ; with this worde, 1046, 1085 ; at oo word(e), 257 f (: lorde *n. nom.*). In the last example the several authorities are at one in writing -*e*.

yren (A.S. īren, *n.*), *nom.*, 1446 ; of yren, 1466, 1498 ; of
. . . . yren, 1431, 1445, 1482.
yse (A.S. īs, *n.*), of yse, 1130.

The five Anglo-Saxon kinship nouns in -*r*, *fæder*, *mōdor*, *brōðor*, *sweostor*, *dohtor*, —

fader (A.S. fæder, *m.*), *nom.*, 194 ; *acc.*, 168 ; ffader, *acc.*, 442.
moder (A.S. mōdor, *f.*), *nom.*, 1983.
brother (A.S. brōðor, *m.*), *nom.*, 2101 f ; *voc.*, 795 f, 816 f.

> Rhyme word. — other *pro*.

suster (A.S. sweostor, *f.*), *nom.*, 1547 ; *acc.*, 419 ; on hir suster, 367.
doghtre (A.S. dohtor, *f.*), That kynges doghtre [was] of Trace, 391. P C T show *was*, and also spell -*er*.

§ 19. The following nouns of Germanic origin, which have no substantives to represent them in Anglo-Saxon, end in *H. F.* in a consonant :

A-bood (cf. A.S. abīdan, *vb.*), of A-bood, 1963.
basket (etym. dub.), amonge a basket, 1687.
bush (cf. O.N. būskr, būski, O.H.G. busc), withouten . . . . bush, 485.
caste (O.N. kasta, *vb.*, kǫstr, *m.*), *acc.*, 1178.
kep(e) (cf. A.S. cēpan, *vb.*), *acc.*, 437 f (: slepe *3 sg. pt. ind.*).
look(e) (cf. A.S. lōcian, *vb.*), *nom.*, 657 f (: at another booke).
pot(-ful) (etym. dub. ; cf. L.G., Du., Dan., Fr. pot), *acc.*, 1686.
skyll(e) (O.N. skil, *n.*), 726 f (: wille *1 sg. pr. ind.*). B C T lack -*e*, but it may be that we should follow F B and retain it.
stroke (cf. A.S. strīcan, *vb.*), withe the stroke, 779.
swogh (cf. A.S. swōgan, *vb.*), *acc.*, 1031 f (: y-nogh *adv.*) ; for the swough, 1941.
tydynge, see § 15.
vnhappe (A.S. un + O.N. happ, *n.*), fro vnhappe, 89.

§ 20. In Romance nouns final -*e* (-*e* mute) is usually retained, both in writing and in sound, except for the regular elision. But there are a good many exceptions, in some of which the -*e* is preserved in writing but loses its value as a syllable, in others of which the -*e* is neither written nor pronounced. (Cf. Child, § 19 ; ten Brink, §§ 222, 223).

For details see the following sections (§§ 21–31). — § 21. Miscellaneous Romance nouns in *-e* which sometimes or always retain *-e* in *H. F.* — § 22. Exceptions to § 21. — § 23. *-aunce.* — § 24. *-ence.* — § 25. *-esse.* — § 26. *-ice.* — § 27. *-ure.* — § 28. *-ère.* — § 29. *chambre, ordre,* etc. — § 30. *-ȳe, -ìe.* — § 31. *contràrye, stòry,* etc.

§ 21. Miscellaneous Romance nouns in *-e* (*-e* mute) which sometimes or always retain *-e* in *H. F.* A few words which have no direct French etymons are included in this list.

acord*e*, 1964. — age, 1986 f (: cage *n.*). — arryvage, 223 f (Cartage *pr. n.*). — Aryvayle, 451 f (: Itayle *pr. n.*). — bataylle, 1447 f (: faille *n.*). — bawm*e*, 1686. — bible, 1334 f (: impossible *adj.*). — cage, 1985 f (: age *n.*). — càrbuncl*e*, 1363. — cause, 369, 747, 1543, 1563, 1875, 1885; caus*e*, 20, 52, 612. — cav*e*, 70, 1584. — charge, 1439 f (: large *pred. adj. sg.*). — compleynt[e], 924 f (: dreynt *3 sg. pt. ind.*); compleynt (+ *cons.*), *362. — cornëmusë and, 1218. — cot*e* (armure), 1326. — couercle, 792 f (: sercle *n.*). — crevace, 2086 f (: pace *inf.*). — crowne, 1825 f (: sowne *inf.*). — cubite, 1370 f (: lyte *pred. adj. sg.*). — disese, 89 f (: plese *inf.*). — doute, 598 f, 2005 f (*both :* aboute *adv.*), 1037 f (: route *inf.*). — Egle, 499, 501, 991, 1110, 1990; Egl*e*, 529. — entent[e], 2000 f, 2132 f (*both* : went *3 sg. pt.*). — ese, 1753 f (: plese *inf.*), 1767 f (: lese *n.*); es*e*, 1750, 2020. — fable, 1479 f (: fauorable *adj.*). — face, 139, 1402, 925 f (: place *n.*). — faille, 188 f, 1448 f; fayle, 429 f.

Rhyme words. — Itayle (188, 429), bataye, *n.* (1448). —

Fame (fame), 305 f, 663 f, 821 f, 1146 f, 1200 f, 1276 f, 1311 f, 1406 f, 1412 f, 1461 f, 1473 f, 1490 f, 1555 f, 1609 f, 1619 f, 1695 f, 1715 f, 1735 f, 1762 f, 1815 f, 1848 f, 1872 f, 1899 f, 2111 f; 349, 844, 1023, 1070, 1560, 1662, 1674, 1709, 1712, 1728, 1836, 1902; Fam*e* (fam*e*), 703, 1404, 1436, 1485, 1502, 1510, 1545, 1617, 1852. In 1105 there may be apocope of *-e*: The Hous of Fame for to descryve. But C lacks *for*, and this is probably the correct reading.

Rhyme words. — game *n.* (663, 821, 1200, 1473), shame *n.* (1815), Dame *n.* (1848), name (the rest). —

famyne, 1974 f (: ruyne *n.*). — flaumb*e*, 769. — flowt*e*, 1223. — fors, see § 22. — fortune, 1547 f (: in comune); fortun*e*, 2016. — grace, 85 f, 240 f, 661 f, 1087 f, 1586 f, 1790 f, 2007 f; grace, 1550; grac*e*, 1537.

Rhyme words. — place *n.* (85, 661, 1087), Trace *pr. n.* (1586, 1790), pace *inf.* (240), solace *inf.* (2007). —

herbe, 290 f (: proverbe *n.*). — heremyte, 659 f (: lyte *pred. adj. sg.*). — Ile, 416 f (: while *n.*) ; yle, 440 f (: Cybile *pr. n.*). — Iape, 414 f (: escape *inf.*) ; Iape, 96. — Ioye, 156 f, 1471 f (*both :* Troye *pr. n..*) ; ioy[e], 83, 1833. — langàge, 861. — laude, 1575 f (: hiraude *inf.*) ; lawde, 1796 f (: Isaude *pr. n.*) ; Laude, 1673. — laure, 1107. — madame (Dame), 1553, 1842, 1863, 1847 f (: fame *n.*). — merite, 669 f (: queyte *inf.*), 2019 f (: lyte *pred.. adj. sg.*). — Muse, 1399. — noyse, 1927 f (: oyse *pr. n.*) ; noyse, 1058 ; noyse, 783, 819, 1521 ; noyse, 1931, 2141. — oure, 1157 f (poure *inf.*). — peple, 360, 1745 ; pepil, 1283. — peyne, 232 f, 312 f (*both :* pleyne *inf.*) ; payne, 1118 f (: spayne *pr. n.*) ; peyn[e], 1570. — pilgrimage, 116. — place, 86 f, 662 f, 719 f, 842 f, 852 f, 926 f, 1088 f, 1111 f, 1163 f, 1169 f, 1237 f, 1356 f, 1459 f, 1956 f, 2041 f, 2092 f ; 1893, 1914, 1996 ; placë hye, 1133 ; place, 834, 836, 843, 1047, 1115.

> Rhyme words. — pace *inf.* (719, 842, 852, 1956, 2092), pace *1 sg. pr. subj.* (1111), pace *1 sg. pr. ind.* (1356), grace *n.* (86, 662, 1088), space *n.* (1237, 2041), face *n.* (926), compace *n.* (1169), deface *inf.* (1163), stace *pr. n.* (1459). —

pouche, 1349. — pouèrte, 88. — preve, 989 f (beleve *inf.*) ; prevef (B P T *end in* -e), 878. — proverbe, 289 f (: herbe *n.*). — Realme, 704. — rethorike, 859 f (: lyke *inf.*). — roche, 1116 f (: aproche *inf.*) ; roche, 1123 ; roche, 1130. — route, 1703 f (: loute *inf.*), 1823 f, 2119 f (*both :* aboute *adv.*) ; route, 1771. — ruyne, 1974 f (: famyne *n.*). — Secte, 1432. — sir (+ *vowel*), 643. — space, 1054 f, 1238 f, 2042 f (*all :* place *n.*). — stewe (cf. O.F. estuve), 26. — table, 1278. — terme, 392. — trone, 1384 ; trone, 1397. — trumpe, 1240, 1670, 1672, 1865 ; trumpe, 1624, 1637, 1678, 1765.

§ 22. Exceptions to § 21.

best (O.F. beste), 1003 (+ *vowel*). — broche (O.F. broche), 1740. — Fantome (O.F. fantosme), 493 ; affaintome, *11. — fors (O.F. force), 999, 1011, 1910, — only in expression *no fors*, and in every case before consonants. — garlande (O.F. garlande), 135. — magìke (O.F. magique), 1269 f (: syke *pred. adj. sg.*) ; màgike(s), 1266. — marvàylle (O.F. merveille), 1372 ; but P C T show a verse without this word. — pelet (O.F. pelote, pilote), 1643 (+ *vowel*). — poete (O.F. poete), 1499 ; poète, 1483. The last verse is harsh, however it be read. — pres (O.F. presse), 167 f (: Anchises), 1633 f (gilteles *adv.*) ; prees, 1358, 1359 f (: dees *n.*). — sours (O.F. sourse), + *vowel*, 544, 551. — tempest (O.F. tempeste),

+ *vowel*, 435, 1036 ; + *consonant*, 220, 221 ; tempest*e*, 209.
— See also *prayer, ryver,* § 28.

§ 23. Nouns in *-aunce, -ance.*

This ending does not occur before a consonant in *H.F.* All rhyme-words are given except nouns in *-aunce.*
acustumaunce, 28 f. — daunce, 639 f (: avaunce *inf.*). — distaunce, 18 f. — dysordynaunce, 27 f. — gouernaunce, 945 f (: launce *inf.*), 958 f.— myschaunce, 957 f.— remembrance, 1182 f. — signifiaunce, 17 f. — substance, 1181 f ; sùbstaunc*e*, 768.

§ 24. Nouns in *-ence.*

This ending always rhymes with itself. In the single example before a consonant there is apocope of *-e*. (Cf. ten Brink, § 223).
abstinenc*e*, 20 ; Abstynenc*e*, 660. — advertence, 709 f. — Apparence, 265 f. — cadence, 623 f. — diligence, 1099 f. — dispence, 260 f. — existence, 266 f. — experience, 788 ; experience, 878 f. — reuerence, 260 f, 624 f, 1426 f. — scìenc*e*, 1091. — sentence, 710 f, 776 f, 877 f, 1100 f, 1425 f ; sentenc*e*, 757. — violence, 775 f.

§ 25. (I.) Abstract nouns in *-esse.* (II.) Feminine nomina agentis in *-esse.*

Nouns in *-esse* commonly rhyme with nouns in *-esse, -nesse.* All other rhyme-words are indicated. In the single example before a consonant *-e* is omitted.
I. distresse, 26 f, 2012 f, 1589 f (: presse *inf.*). — gentilesse, 1611 f (: blesse *3 sg. pr. subj.*). — humblesse, 630 f (: blesse *3 sg. pr. subj.*). — làrges (+ *cons.*), 1309 (*bis*). — noblesse, 471 f, 1424 f, 971 f (: Boesse *pr. n.*). — Richesse, 472 f ; richesse, 1393 f ; rychesse, 1423 f ; ryches (F *alone lacks* -e), 1416 f. — For convenience *tresse* (O.F. tresce), 230 f, is included in this list.
II. godesse, 1394 f ; goddes (F *alone lacks* -e), 1415 f ; goddess*e*, 1406. — hunteresse, 229 f (: tresse *n.*).

§ 26. Nouns in *-yce, -yse.*

There is apocope of *-e* in the single example before a consonant.
Iustice, 1820 f (: vice *n.*). — seruys*ẹ*, 626. — vice, 276 f (: nyce *adj.*), 1819 f (: Iustice *n.*) ; vic*e* (*so* C T ; F B *vices, monosyl.*, which is impossible), 1834.

§ 27. Nouns in *-ure*.

For apocope, see *parauenture*, 792 ; for *-ë* before a consonant, see *auentur[e]*, 2090. Except as indicated, nouns in the following list rhyme only with each other.

armure (cote armure), 1326 f. — auenture, 463 f, 1297 f, 1982 f (: endure *inf.*) ; auentur[e], 2090 ; auenture, 1052 ; perauenture, 304 f (: dure *3 sg. pr. subj.*) ; parauenture, 792 ; parauenture, 1997. — creature, 489 f, 1365 f, 2040 f. — cure, 464 f, 1298 f. — figure, 132 f. — nature, 490 f, 1366 f, 2039 f. — portreytoure, 132 f. — vesture, 1325 f.

§ 28. Nouns in *-ere*.

Here for convenience are put *chere, manere, matere, prayer, ryver*,—the last two showing no *-e*.

chere, 179 f, 671 f (*both :* here *inf.*), 214 f (: dere *adj. voc. post.*), 277 f (: manere *n.*), 1743 f (: bere *n.*) ; chere, 154.

manere, 249 f (: fere *n.*), 278 f (: chere *n.*), 1729 f (: dere *adj. voc. post.*). —màner, *before consonants*, 489, 509, 670, 1123, 1219, 1524 ; *before vowels*, 126, 1197, 1699 ; *before h*, 375. For the most part, *maner* is used in such phrases as *no maner creature, euery maner man, somme maner thinge*, etc. The exceptions are 126, 1197, 375, — the first two before vowels, the last before *h*.

matere, 861 f, 1517 f (*both :* here *inf.*), 1013 f (: here *adv.*), 1126 f (: clere *adv.*) ; màtere, 637.

pràyer, 107 (+ *cons.*), 465 (+ *vowel*).

Rỳuer, 748 (+ *cons.*) ; rỳver, 1653 (+ *cons.*).

§ 29. Nouns in consonant + *-re*.

chambre, 366. — Decembre, 63 f (: remembre *inf.*) ; Dècembrè, 111. — foudre (F *founder*), 535 f (: poudre *n.*). — ordre, 1453 ; ordrë (+ *vowel*), 1905. — poudre (F *powder*), 536 f (: foudre *n.*) ; poudre, 1644. — sklaundre, 1625 ; sklaundre, 1580. — soulfre, 1508.

§ 30. Nouns in *-ỳe, -ìe*.

When the ending rhymes with itself, the rhyme-words are left unregistered.

Armonye, 1396 f. — cheualrie, 1340 f (: asye *pr. n.*). — companye, 1551 f (: lye *n.*), 1607 f, 1727 f (*both :* crie *inf.*), 1657 f (: hye *inf.*), 1690 f (: aspye *inf.*), 1811 f ; companye, 1528. — envye, 95 f, 1476 f (: espie *inf.*). — fantasye, 593 f (: espye *inf.*), 992 f (: crye *inf.*). — folye, 1972 f. — Galoxie, 936 f (: ye *n.*). — Ielousye, 1971 f. — maistrye, 1094 f (: gye *inf.*). — melodye, 1395 f. — navye, 216 f (: an hye). — philosophie, 857 f; Philosophye, 974 f (: hye *adv.*). — poetrie, 858 f, 1001 f (: stellifye *inf.*). — trayterye, 1812 f. — tresorye, 524. — vilanye, 96 f. — Observe also *perrë* (O.F. pierrerie), 124 ;, *perry* (*slur*), 1393.

§ 31. Nouns in unaccented -*ye*.

contrarye, 808 f (: varye *1 sg. pr. ind.*) ; contraire, 1540 f (: faire *adv.*) ; contrairie, 1629 f (: fayre *adv.*). — lapidaire, 1352 f (: faire *adj. def. post. pl.*). — story (*slur*), 149 ; story (+ *cons.*), 406. — studye (-*ye slurred*), 30 ; studye (+ *cons.*, *dissyl.*), 633.

§ 32. A few Romance words that end in a consonant in Old French take a final -*e* in *H. F.*

Beryle (O.F. beril), 1184 f (: Gyle *pr. n.*). — compace (O.F. compas), 1170 f (: place *n.*) ; *but* còmpas, 462 f (: Eneas *pr. n.*), 798 f (: was *3 sg. pt. ind.*). — pale (O.F. pal), 1840 f (: tale *n.*). — trauaylle (O.F. travail), 1750 f (: avyalle *inf.*). — Note also *in comune* (O.F. comun, *adj.*), 1548 f (: Fortune *n.*).

§ 33. Words ending in Old French in -*é* and -*ée* end indiscriminately in -*e* in *H.F.* (See ten Brink, § 223, V.).

Gothic figures indicate that a vowel follows without causing elision.

auctoritè, 2158 f. — beaùte, **533**, 1172 ; beautè, 1177 f. — bountè, 1698 f. — charytè, 108 f. — Citèe, 1845 f; Citèe, 2080. — Contrèe, 146 f, 241 f; contrèe, 475 f, 647 f ; contrè, 2135 f ; Còntree, **196**; còntree, **224**; còntree highte, **1585**. — curiositè, 1178 f. — destanèe, 145 f; destanỹe (*trisyl.*), 188. — facultè, 248 f. — Iolytèe, **682**. — meynèe, 194 f, 933 f. — pìtee, 180, **316**; pitèe, 325 f ; pitè, 412 f. — plènte, **1973**. — prolixitè, 856 f. — subtilitè, 855 f. — suèrte, **723**. — tretèe 453 f. — For *valèy*[e] (O.F. valée), cf. 1918 f (: sey *inf.*). — For *pardè*, cf. 404 f, 575 f, 840 f, 860, 1896 f ; *pàrdee*, 1000, 1032.

§ 34. Romance nouns which have no final -*e* in French have none in *H. F.* (A few Latin words are included in this section).

For convenience the examples are classed as, — (I.) words in -*er ;* (II.) words in -*our ;* (III.) words in -*ent*, -*ment ;* (IV.) words in -*ion*, -*ioun ;* (V.) words in -*s ;* (VI.) words in a vowel ; (VII.) miscellaneous words.

I. Words in -*er*.

botiller (Norm. F. butuiller), 592 f. — corner (O.F. cornier), 1052. — messanger (O.F. messagier), 1583, 1591; messangere, 1568. — mouer, 81. — pìler (O.F. piler, pilier), 1428, 1430, 1457, 1486, 1491, 1497, 1507; pelèr, 1421 f (: clere *pred. adj. sg.*); pilèr(e), 1443 f (: here *adv.*), 1465 f (: Omere *pr. n.*), 1481 f (clere *adj. post. sg.*). It can hardly be that -*e*, which several times appears in rhyme, is in any case sounded. — porter (O.F. portier), 1954.

II. Words in -*our*.

auttour, 314. — fauour, 1688, 1788; fauor (*fautor*), 519. — hònour, 635, 1416; honoùr, 1611, 1752 f, 1793 f. — làbour, 652, 666, *1962; laboùr, 1751 f, 1794 f. — Rasour, 690. — Sygamour, 1278 f. — traytour, 267. — tregetour, 1278 f. —

III. Words in -*ent*, -*ment*.

accident, 1976 f. — comaundëment, 612 f, 2021 f. — element, 976 f. — entendëment, 983 f. — fundament, 1132 f. — misgouernëment, 1975 f. —tùrment, 445.

IV. Words in -*ion*, -*ioun*.

avisioun, 7 f; avision, 104 f; a Visyon, 513 f. — clarioun, 1573 f, 1579 f, 1723 f, 1801 f, 1818 f; claryoun, 1241 f; clarion, 1247 f. — conclusion, 103 f; conclusyon, 342 f, 848 f, 871 f. — condicioun, 1904 f. — congregacioun, 2034 f. — contemplacion, 33 f; contemplacioun, 1710 f. — demonstracion, 727 f. — descripsion, 987 f; descripcioun, 1903 f. — destruction, 151 f. — deuocion, 33 f, 68 f, 494 f, 666 f. — disposicioun, 2113 f. — duracioun, 2114 f. — entencion, 93 f. — Illusion, 493 f. — Inuocacion, 67 f. — mansyon, 754 f; mansion, 831 f. — mensyon, 56 f. — multiplicaciovn(e), 784 f; multiplicacion, 820 f. — nacion, 207 f. — oppinion, 55 f. — persuasion, *872. — presumpcion, 94. — recompensacion, 665 f, 1557 f. — Region, 431 f, 929; region, 988 f; Regioun, 1641 f. — reuelacioun, 8 f. — savacion, 208. — Scorpioun, 948 f. — ymagynacion, 728 f.

V. Words in -*s*.

apocalips, 1385 f. — caas, 254 f, 578; cas(e), 1052 f (: pace *n.*). — compas, see § 32. — dees, 1360 f, 1421, 1658. — encres, 2074 f. — loos, 1620, 1621, 1626, 1722, 1817, 1859, 1900, 1965, 1667 f. — pac(e), 1051 f (: case *n.*). — paleys, 713, 1075, 1090. — paradys, 918 f. — pes, 1961. — processe, 251. — purpos, 377 f. — trespas, 428 f. — vois, 556, 561, 563; voys, 819. — For rùbee (O.F. rubis), see 1362.

VI. Words ending in a vowel (not -*e*).

affrày, 553 f. — arrày, 228 f. — mèrcy, 1730 ; mercỳ, 1874 f. — nèviwẹ, 617. — prow(e) (O.F. prou), 579 f (: nowe *adv.*). — vèrtu, 526, 550, 631, 1101 ; vertùe, 1851. — For *parfey(e)*, see 938 f (: weye *n.*).

VII. Miscellaneous.

airẹ, 718, 779, 908 ; air*e*, 770, 775, 1041 ; air(e), 768 f (: faire *pred. adj. sg.*) ; ayrẹ, 816 ; ayr*e*, 811, 813, 817 ; ayr(e), 834 f (: faire *pred. adj. sg.*) ; eyrẹ, 927 ; eyr*e*, 765, 954. — Art, 1095 ; art(e), 335 f, 627 f, 1882 f (*all :* parte *n.*) ; artẹ, 1276. — Citezyn, 930 f.— Còrseynt, 117.— delyt*e*, 1831 ; delyt(e), 309 f (: profite *n.*). — dèsert, 488. — dispitẹ, 1716 ; dispit*e*, 96, 1668. — ducat, 1348. — duk*e*, 388. — effectẹ, 5. — engỳn*e*, 528 (*skill*), 1934 (*machine*). — fool, 958. — frot, 2017. — ffugityf*e*, 146. — gebet, 106. — guerdon, 619. — hostel(e), 1022 f (: wele *adv.*).— metal, 1422, 1446.— ost(e), 186 f (: goste *n.*). — part, 344 ; part(e), 366 f, 628 f, 1881 f (*all :* arte *n.*). — point, 917, 2018. — prison, 26. — profit(e), 310 f (: delyte *n.*). — renoun, 1736, 1558 f, 1709 f, 1817 f, renovn(e), 1850 f (: tovne *n.*) ; rènoun, 1406.— rèson, 708 ; reason, 753 f ; reasoun, 761 f. — roundell, 791 ; roundel, 798. — ryban, 1318. — seson, 341 f. — skorn*e*, 95. — soun, 824, 762 f, 832 f, 847 f, 1025 f, 1239 f, 1574 f, 1642 f, 1724 f, 1802 f ; sovnẹ, 720, 773. 1805 ; sovn(e), 742 f (: doun *adv.*), 783 f (: multiplicaciovne *n.*) ; sovn*e*, 765, 770, 1033, 1950. — spiritẹ, 190. — stryf(e), 1964 f (: lyfe *n.*). — tour*e*, 536 ; tour(e), 1185 f (: bure *n.*). — tuell(e), 1649 f (: welle *adv.*). — vessel, 2130. — wiket, 477.

> Note. — In none of the foregoing words is -*e* sounded, though some of them have this ending regularly (*aire, arte, parte*, etc.) and others show no other form (*delyte, dispite, profite*, etc.). Within the verse there is always apocope or elision, and when final the rhyme-word shows the -*e* illegitimate.

§ 35. The genitive singular of nouns, whether of Germanic or Romance origin, ends in *H. F.* for the most part in -*es* (variants -*is*, -*ys*), irrespective of original gender and declension.

Examples are : —

I. domes, 1284. — Egles (F B *lack the line*), 507. — folkes, see § 44. — goddis, 1384, 1799 ; goddes, 1711, 1758 ; goddys, 1697. — houses, 1959. — kynges, 391. — loues, 645, 675,

1489. — mannes, 556. — sonnes, 941. — soules, 408. — wor[l]des 1867. — yates, 1302.

> Note 1. — For *alle skynnes* (alles kynnes), cf. 1530; *no skynnes* (nones kynnes), 1794.
>
> Note 2. — In the phrase *lives body* (1063), Skeat (*Minor Poems, Glossary*) regards *lives* as an adverb. Bright (*M. L. N.*, 1889, col. 363) explains the phrase as "a living person's body", "a living man." Kittredge's interpretation (*Language of Chaucer's Troilus*, § 35, I, n.) that *lives* means "of life" (cf. Byron's "a thing of life"; "As thou art a man of life," *Little Musgrave and Lady Barnard*, A, st. 10, Child, *Ballads*, II, 244) is, however, more satisfactory as explaining also the parallel expressions *lyues creature, lyues man*, found elsewhere in Chaucer. Thus lives body = body of life = living body = living man.

II. Fames, fames, 786, 852, 882, 1027, 1357, 1603, 1857. — Philosophres, 758. — tigres, 1459. — trumpes, 1642, 1646, 1685.

§ 36. One word makes a genitive without change of form:

Fader carte, 943; but C T here show *-s*.

> Note. — In *heuen kynge* (1084), *heuen* is probably in composition and not a real genitive (cf. A.S. heofon-cyning). Observe further *heuens region* (988), *heuens sygnes* (998). In both of these examples B has *heuenys*. — In the phrase *wounde smerte* (374), Skeat (*Minor Poems, Glossary*) sets *smerte* down as a noun, which would of course make *wounde* genitive. But *smerte* seems rather an adjective here, as also in the parallel expression *sorwes smerte* (316). (Cf. Kittredge, § 67, *n.*).

§ 37. Genitives of proper names.

I. Of names in *-s* but three examples have been noted in the genitive. Two of these have the genitive like the nominative, — Eaycedis chiron, 1206; Venus clerk, 1487; the third forms genitive in *-es*, — Martes metal, 1446.

II. Other genitives.

Arionis harp, 1005. — Athalantes Doughtres, 1007. — Auffrikes Region, 431. — Iupiter[e]s wife, 199. — Romes myghty werkes, 1504.

§ 38. The plural of nouns, of whatever origin, ends regularly in *-es* (*-ys, -is*). (Cf. Child, § 22; ten Brink, §§ 202, 206, 210, 213, 225).

I. acordes, 695 f. — Actes, 347. — apes, 1806 f. — aqueyntaunces, 694 f. — armes, 144, 1331, 1337, 1411. — ascendentes,

1268 f. — auentures, 47 f, 1631 f. — rabewyures (*l.* babewynnes), 1189. — berdys, 689. — bàtaylès, 454; batàyles, 1441 f. — beres, 1589. — bestes, 900 f, 932, 965 f, 1383, 1390, 1968 f; bestis, 1226. — bildynges, 1966 f. — biles, 868 f. — bokes, 385; bookys, 622. — boystes, 2129. — bromes, 1226 f. — brynkes, 803. — cages, 1938. — causes, 13; causis, 19 f (: caus*e* is). — charmeresses, 1261 f. — chidynges, 1028 f. — chirkynges, 1943 f. — clerkes, 1265, 1503 f; clerkys, 53 f, 760. — clothes, 1319. — cloudes, 966. — compàsses, 1302. — compassinges, 1188 f. — cordes (F B *acordes*), 696 f. — cornes, 698.— corovnes, 1317.—creatures, 1632 f.— Daunces, 1235.— dìscordès (C T *dìscordęs*), 685. — dores, 480, 1420, 1952; dor[e]s, 650 f (: neygh[e]bor[e]s). — dowves, 137. — dremes, 35. — eles, 2154 f. — ententes, 1267 f. — eres, 879, 1389 f. — eschaunges, 697 f. — fames, 1139, 1154 f, 1233, 1292. — feldès, 897. — festes, 1222. — figùres, 48 f, 126 f; fìgurès, 858. — flakes, 1192.— florisshinges, 1301 f.— forestes 899 f. — foules, 1382. — frenges, 1318 f. — furtherynges, 636 f. — gendres, 18. — gestes (*res gestae*), 1434, 1515 f, 1518, 1737 f. — goddess(e), 172; goddes, 1002; goddys, 460. — graunges, 698 f. — Grekes, 1479. — greses, 1353. — greyn(d)es, 691.— gromes, 1225 f.— gyges, 1942.— habitacles, 1194 f. — hattes, 1940. — hayles, 967. — heles 2153 f. — herau(l)des, 1321 f. — heres, 1390 f. — hillès (*or* hìllęs), 898. — holes, 1949, 2110. — hondes, 299, 692 f. — Iangles, 1960 f. — Iapes, 1805 f. — ioynynges, 1187 f. — kervynges, 1302 f. — knyghtis, 455 f. — kyndes, 204 f, 968 f. — kynges, 1316 f. — laudes, 1322 f. — lestes, 1738 f. — leues, 1946. — leysinges, 676 f; lesenges, 2123 f. — loses, 1688 f. — losynges, 1317 f. — loues, 677. 678, 679, 697; louès (*or* louęs), 86. — mariages, 1961 f — meracles, 12 f. — mervayles, 1442 f. — mountaynes, 898 f. — mynstralles, 1197 f. — mystes, 966. — names, 1137, 1142, 1153 f, 1355, 1505. — nayles, 542. — nestes, 1516 f. — neygh[e]bor[e]s, 649 f (: dor[e]s). — novchis, 1350 f (: povch*e* is). — oracles, 11 f. — oures, 689 f. — peces, 1187. — Phitonesses, 1261. — pilgrimes, 2122 f. — pipes, 1224. — places, 1014. — playnes, 897 f. — portreytures, 125 f. — preysynges, 635 f. — pursevantes, 1321. — pynacles, 124 f, 1189 f, 1193 f. — rekenynges, 653 f. — renoveilaunces, 693 f. — reynes (*rein*), 951. — reynes (*rain*), 967. — roches, 1035. — roses, 1687 f. — ryghtis, 456 f. — ryvèr[e]s, 901. — sheves, 2140. — shippes, 195, 233, 365, 903, 1036. — shrippes, 2123. — Sisoùres, 690 f, — skilles, 750, 867 f. — sondes, 691 f. — sones, 75 f (: won*e* is). — songes, 622, 1396. — Sorceresses, 1262. — sprynges, 1235 f, 1984 f.— stages, 122 f.— sterlynges, 1315 f.— sterres, 993, 1254, 1376.— stones, 1351.— strondes, 148.— strynges, 777. — syght[es], 2010. — sygnes, (F B *sygnẹs*), 998. — tabernacles, 123 f, 1190 f. — tales, 1198 f. — techches, 1778 f.— tempestes, 966 f, 1967 f. — termes, 857. — theves, 1779. — thynges, 643 f, 654 f, 674, 743, 1236 f, 1889, 1893 f, 2057 ; thinges, 2009 f. — tonges, 1390. — tovnes, 902. — twigges, 1936 ; twy(n)ges, 1941 f. —tydynges, 644 f, 675 f, 1027 f, 1894 f, 1907 f (: brynges *2 sg. pr. ind.*), 1957 f, 1983 f, 2010 f, 2124 f ; tydẏngës (*or* tẏdyngẹs), 1888 ; tẏdyngẹs. 1955, 2143 ; tẏdyngịs, 1886. — tymes, 19, 1216, 2121 f, 2:26, — viages, 1962 f. — walles, 1288, 1398. — werkes, 54 f, 1504 f, 1610, 1616, 1696, 1707 (F B *werkẹs*) ; werkès (*or* werkẹs), 1701.; werkẹs, 1666, 1720. — wisprynges, 1958 f. — wordes, 191, 311, 376, 572. — wrecches (*l.* wicches), 1262. — wrechches, 1777 f. — wyndes, 203 f, 246, 967 f, 1587, *1967. — wynges, 922, 1392. — wynnynges, 1965 f. — ymàges, 121 f, 1269 ; ẏmagès, 472.

II.   dayes, 695. — weyes, 585, 1122. — *Also* reyes (F B *reus*), 1236. — valey[e]s, 899.

III.   (*a*) clawes, 545, 554 ; clowes, 1785 f. — sawes, 676. — shrewes, 1830, 1833 f, 1852 f. — snowes, 967, 1192 f. — thewes, 1834 f, 1851 f. — wyndowes, 1191. — (*b*) morwes, 4. — sorwes, 316, 467. — *Also* Iowes, 1786 f. — mowes, 1806. — pawes, 541.

IV.   Angles, 1959 f. — Doughtres, 1007. — evẹnes, 4 f. — fethẹres, 974, 1382 ; fethres (F B *lack the line*), 507 ; Fethres, 530. — lettres, 1141, 1144. — nobles, 1315. — shuldres, 1410, 1435, 1462, 1500 — swevenes, 3 f. — wondres, 1996, 2118.

V.   lẏës (*lies*), 1477 f, 2129 f. — lẏës (*lees*), 2130 f. — màsonẹrïës, 1303 f. — mènstralcïës, 1217 f. — nòuelrïës, 686 f. — pïës, 703 f. — Pòetrïës, 1478 f. — shalmẏës, 1218 f. — spïës, 704 f. — ymàgerẏës (F *lacks the line*), 1304 f. — *With synizesis* ymàgerïẽs, 1190.

VI.   (*a*) glèës, 1209 f, 1252 f (*both* : sèës *n. pl.*). — knèës, 1534, 1772 ; *but* knes, 1659, 1705. — sèës, 1210 f, 1251 f (*both*.: glèës *n. pl.*). — trèës, 752, 1516, 902 f (: Citèës *n. pl.*), 1946 f (: entrèës *n. pl.*).— (*b*) Citèës, 901 f (: trèës *n. pl.*). — entrèës, 1945 f (: trèës *n. pl.*).

§ 39.   Exceptions to § 38. The following words ending in a consonant or an accented -*e* sometimes or always make their

plural in -s (-z), -ęs, or -is. (Cf. Child, § 22 ; ten Brink, § 226).
I. Words in -nt.
Instrumentęs, 696. — servantęs, 625.
II. Words in -ion, -ioun.
Avisions, 40 f ; avisions, 48. — clarions, 1597 ; Clarioun[s], 1594. — complexions, 21 f. — condiciouns, 1530 f. — dissymulacions, 688 f. — exorsisacions, 1263 f. — fumi(y)gacions, 1264 f. — impressions, 39 f. — reflexions, 22 f. — regiouns, 1529 f ; Regions, 1970 f. — reparacions, 688 f. — transmutacions, 1969 f.
III. Words in -r.
coloùrs, 859. — currours, 2128. — dossèrs, 1940 f. — gestiours, 1198. — harpers, 1207, 1209. — Iugelours, 1259 f. — louers, 37. — messangers, 2128 f. — murmuręs, 686. — pànyèrs, 1939 f. — Pardoners, 2127 f. — pipers, 1234. — tregetours, 1260 f. — werręs, 1961.
> Note. — Of the foregoing examples B shows -ys in 686, 859, 1198, 1259, 1260, 1940, 2128. The vowel, however, is manifestly unsounded except in 859, where we may well read *coloùrỳs* for *coloùrs*.

IV. Words in -en.
magiciens, 1260. — troyèns, 156.
V. Miscellaneous words with consonantal ending.
corbetz (P T *corbettęs*, C *corbettis*), 1304. — estatęs, 1970. — restęs, *1962. — rovnyngęs (C *Rownyng*), 1960. — signàls, 459 f. — spìritis (C T *spirìtis*), 41. — wellęs, *1984. — Cf. also, *hilles, tydynges, werkes*, § 38, above.
VI. dytees (*dissyl.*), 622 f (: lyt*e* is). In this verse F B have *dytees bookys*, but the rhyme-word shows clearly that *bookys dytees* is the proper order. — For *knèës, knes*, see § 38, VI, *a*, above.

§ 40. Plurals of the *n*-declension which preserve the Anglo-Saxon ending (-*an*) in the form -*en* are :
been (A.S. *pl.* bēon, Ps. bīan), 1522.
eyen (A.S. *pl.* ēagan, L. æʒen, eʒen, P.Pl[a]. eʒen, eiʒen, P.Pl[b]. eyghen, eyghes, P.Pl[c]. eyen), 459 1379, 1408 ; yen, 1381, 2152 (B *correctly* nose and yen ; F noyse an highen).
foon (A.S. *pl.* gefān) not found ; *but* foos, 1668 f (: loos *n.*).
toon (A.S. *pl.* tān), 2028 f (: anoon *adv.*), — *so* C ; T *ton(e)*, F B *lack the verse*.

§ 41. Plurals in *-en* by imitation (Child, § 24 ; ten Brink, §§ 215, 217).

sustren (A.S. *pl.* sweoster, L. sustren, sostres, P.Pl^c. sustren, sustres, susteres), 1401.

For *Doughtres*, see § 38.

§ 42. Plurals with umlaut (Child, § 26 ; ten Brink, § 214).

fetẹ (A.S. fēt), 568, 606, 1374, 1391 ; fet(e), 1603 f (: hete *3 sg. pt. ind.*) ; *and with final* -e *sounded* fete, 1050 f (: strete *n.*).

men (A.S. menn), 330, 338, 525, 590, 609, 1326, 1761, etc., etc.

wymmen (A.S. wifmenn, *Pet. Chron.* wimmen), 335, 1741, 1760 ; wommen, 1747.

§ 43. In the following words plurals occur identical in form with the singular.

folke (A.S. folc, *n.*, *pl.* folc). No accurate distinction for singular and plural is possible for this word. In the following examples the verb is plural, — 645, 1060, 1338, 1544, 1608, 1661, 1775, 1832, 1854, 1862, 1899. In one case only is the verb singular, and it is interesting to note the passage to the plural in the succeeding verse :

That alle the folke that *ys* a lyve
Ne *han* the kunnynge to discryve, 2055-6.

Another certain singular is seen in *a folke*, 73. The limiting word indicates a singular in *this folke*, 1544, 1775, 1790, 1862, though in three of the four examples a plural verb follows. For other examples of *folke* in various constructions, cf. 42, 237, 638, 1358, 1849, 1968, 2035, 2138, etc. Final *-e* is regularly written in our MS., and is in one case sounded :

Of loues folkẹ moo tydynges, 675.

Forms in *-es*, *-ys*, also occur (1154, 1426, 1828), but the vowel is uniformly silent.

In the genitive *folkes* (*folkys*) is the regular form, and the vowel is pronounced ; cf. 21, 636, 1137, 1322, 1720.

foote (A.S. fōt, *m.*, *pl.* fēt), XX^{ti}. foote thykke, 1335.

hors (A.S. hors, *n.*, *pl.* hors), 944, 952.

hosẹ (A.S. hosa, *m.*, *pl.* hosan), 1840.

mylẹ (A.S. mīl, *f.*, *pl.* mīla, mīle), sixty mylẹ, 1979 ; *but* myles two, 116.

Swynẹ (A.S. swīn, *n.*, *pl.* swīn), 1777.

thingẹ, thing (A.S. þing, *n.*, *pl.* þing). The following examples are pretty certainly plural :

Other thingẹ to tellen yowe, 1418 ;

As wel of loue as other thyng(e), 1739 f (: rynge *n*.) ;
In allë thing ryght as it is, 1837.

But the regular plural is *thinges* ; see § 38. In the following verse -*s* should doubtless be supplied, though it is nowhere written :

Some newe thingë y not what, 1887.

wyse (A.S. wīse, *f*., *pl*. wīsan) must certainly be plural in the following verses :

But this may be in many wyse
Of which I wil the two deuyse, 771-2 ;
But for to prove in allë wyse, 1347.

§ 44. The genitive plural does not differ in form from the genitive singular.

folkes, see § 43. — goddys botiller, 592. — grekes oste, 186. — Iewes gestes, 1434. — partriches wynges, 1392. — rokes nestes, 1516. — sterres names, 997. — stormes bete, 1150.

§ 45. The dative plural (Anglo-Saxon -*um*) has not been observed in *H.F.*

ADJECTIVES.

§ 46. Adjectives ending in Anglo-Saxon in a short vowel (in the indefinite use) end in -*e* in *H. F.* (Cf. Child, § 29 ; ten Brink, § 230).

Most of these are either *jo*-stems or *i*-stems that have gone over entirely to the *jo*-declension : *blythe, dere, grene, kynde, lythe, newe, shene, stille, swete, thikke, trewe*. So also *vnmerie*. Here belongs *vnsofte*. For *allone*, cf. § 47.

blythe (A.S. blīðe, L.O. blīðe), be thou euer blythe, 1860 f (: swithe *adv*.).

dere (A.S. dēore, W.S. dīere, dȳre, L. deore, dure, O. deore, dere). The only examples are in the definite use : my lady dere, 213 f (: chere *n*.) ; my dere hert[e], 326 ; lady dere, 1730 f (: manere *n*.) ; lady leefe and dere, 1827 f (: here *inf*.).

grene (A.S. grēne, grœne, L. grene), grene corne, 1224.

kynde (A.S. cynde, *but usually* gecynde), As kynde thinge of Fames is, 1292 ; she ys vnkynde, 284 f (: fynde *inf*.). Definite use : hys kynde place, 834, 836.

lythe (A.S. līðe, L. liðe, O. liþe), To make lythe of that was harde, 118. In this verse P omits *of*; CT omit *of* and insert *erst* after *that*. The reading of P seems more likely correct, and this would give us *lythĕ*.

newe (A.S. nēowe, nīowe, W.S. nīewe, nīwe, L. neawe, neouwe, niwe, O. neowe, newe, P.Pl. newe, nywe), That euery yere wolde haue a newe, 302 f (: trewe *adj*.) ; Alle newe of gold another sonne, 506. The last line is seen only in C T.

shene (A.S. scēne, scȳne, scēone, L. sceone, scone, L^b. scene, O. shene, scone). Occurs only in the vocative expression *lady shene*, 1536 f (: quene *n*.).

stille (A.S. stille, L. stille, O. stille, still), he stode as stille as stoon, 1605 ; That neuer mo stil hyt stent[e], *1926. In the last example we should probably read *hyt stille ;* so Willert on the basis of *it styl* in T.

swete (A.S. swēte, swœte, O. swet), floode of helle vnswete, 72 f (: lete *pr. n.*). Definite use : my swete hert, 315.

thikke (A.S. þicce, L. thicke), Or elles was the aire so thikke, 908 f (: prikke *n*.) ; a bible XX^{ti}. foote thykke, 1335.

trewe (A.S. trēowe, W.S. triewe, trȳwe, L. treowe, O. trowwe), is euery man thus trewe, 301 f (: a newe *adj. as subs.*).

vnmerie (A.S. myrige, merge). Only in the definite use : this god vnmerie, 74 f (: Cymerie *pr. n.*).

Vn-softe (A.S. sōfte *adv.*, but also used as *adj.* instead of sēfte, sœfte (cf. Sievers, § 299, n. 1, and Sweet, 2081) L. softe, O. soffte). In the definite use only : the cruelle lyfe Vn-softe, 36 f (: ofte *adj. post. pl.*).

    Note. — For the adj. *free* (A.S. frēo), cf. Anchyses the free, 422 f (: see *inf.*).

§ 47. In *allone*, *-e* goes back to the Anglo-Saxon weak ("definite") ending *-a*.

allone (A.S. eall āna, L. al ane, O. all ane), And eke allone (*plur.*) be hem selue, 2125 ; Deserte allone (*sing.*) || ryghte in the se, 416.

§ 48. *Lyte, muche* belong in a category by themselves. On their relations to A.S. lȳt, lȳtel, micel, mycel, see especially Bright, *American Journal of Philology*, IX, 219.

lyte (A.S. lȳt, *adv.*, lȳtel, *adj.*) is said by ten Brink, § 231, to be "im Sing. wohl nur substantivisch gebraucht," but this is contradicted by three places in *H.F.* : *thyn Abstinence ys lyte*, 660 f (: heremyte *n.*), *she was so lyte*, 1369 f (: cubite *n.*), *hyt nas not lyte*, 1978 f (: write *1 sg. pr. ind.*). Cf., also,

Wol do than ese al be hyt lyte, 2020 f (: merite *n.*), where the word may be held a substantive. For the substantive use of *lyte*, see 621, 1349 (F B *litel, monosyl.*), and perhaps 2020. For *lyte*, adv., see 778 f (smyte *3 pl. pr. ind.*).

For *lytel*, see 1093, 1225 ; *litel*, 791 ; *litil*, 1476 ; *lytel*, adv., 1134.

> Note. — Lines 621-2 run as follows :
> Al-though that in thy hede ful lytel is
> To make songes dytees bookys.
> All authorities show *lytel* (in varied spelling). C T, however, shift the position of *dytees, bookys.* Manifestly the proper reading is :
> Al-though that in thy hede ful lyt*e* is
> To make songes bookys dytees.

moche (A.S. micel, L.W.S. mycel), ful moche prees, 1358 ; a[s] moche goode, 1748 ; ful moche pyne, 147 ; moch compleynt, 924 ; moch*e* ys thy myght, 971. — a mochil (*monosyl.* ; P C T *grete*) myschaunce, 957 ; mochel wele, 1138 ; to mochil prees, 1359. For *adverbial use, see* ouer mech*e*, 38 ; moch*e* or lyte, 778 ; as moch*e* as, 1749.

§ 49. Several adjectives which in Anglo-Saxon end in a consonant, sometimes or always take *-e* in *H. F.* (Cf. Child, § 30 ; ten Brink, § 231).

Some of the *-e*'s in the following list are perhaps to be explained on grammatical grounds. Of petrified vocatives (cf. ten Brink, § 235, Anm., but also Zupitza, *Deutsche Litteratur-Zeitung*, 1885, coll. 610, 613, and Freudenberger, pp. 37–40) there is one example : *faire Venus.* Observe the expressions *longe tyme, longe while, olde tyme*, in which, says Manly (*Language of the Legend of Good Women*, § 49), "one is tempted to see the remains of old dative constructions in which the final vowel has been preserved by the cadence of the phrase."

[bare] (A.S. bær, L^a. bare, L^b. bar, P.Pl^{bc}. bare, P.Pl^c. bar), *only in* barefote (A.S. bærfōt, L^a. bar-fot, L^b. bareuot) That dreme he barefote dreme he shod, 98.

[brode] (A.S. brād, L. bræd, brad, brod, O. brad, P.Pl. brod), *only in* brod*e* as a couercle, 792.

faire (A.S. fæger, L. fæir, fæire, fæiȝer, faire, O. faȝȝerr, P.Pl. fayre), And faire Venus also, 618. — fair(e), 767 f, 833 f (*both* : aire *n.*) ; feire, 1028 ; far*e*, 1305.

[false] (late A.S. fals, from O.F. or Latin, P.Pl. fals), *no example.* — fals, *before consonant*, 414 ; *before vowels*, 266, 285,

397, 405, 1029, 2108 ; *in rhyme*, 393 f (: hals *n.*), 2072 f (: als *adv.*).

[foul*e*] (A.S. fūl, O. ful), *only in* foul*e* or faire, 766, 833.

goode (A.S. gōd, L.O. god), Lady graunte vs good[e] fame, 1609 (*but* P C T graunte vs *now*) ; That we mowe han as good[e] fame, 1735 (*but* P C T as good *a*) ; Of good[e] folke and gunne crie, 1608 (but we must certainly take this as *plural*). — good*ẹ*, 671, *872 ; good*e*, 604 ; good, 264, 1545, 1555, 1558, 1560, 1617, 1621, 1799, 1815, 1817, 1832, 1854.

grete (A.S. grēat, O. græt), I herde a gretë noys*ẹ* with alle, 2147. But it may be that the verse should read — I herde a gretë noysè with alle. — gret*ẹ*, 24, 26, 806, 856, 1528, 1850, 1973 ; gret*e*, 553, 630, 1927, 2158 ; gret, 1372, 1424, *1425, 1736, 1852.

harde (A.S. heard, L. heard, herd, O. harrd), This Eolus with harde grace, 1586. — hard*ẹ*, 861 ; hard(e), 118 f (: leonarde *pr. n.*) ; hard, 861.

hye (A.S. hēah, M. hēh, L. hæh, hæhӡe, O. heh), That neuer herd I thing so hye (*adv.* ?), 1020 f (: crye *inf.*) ; on a place hye, 1133 f (: glorifye *inf.*) ; so hygh a roche, 1116.— on hy*e*, 1360 ; on high(e), 1430 f (: sighe *3 sg. pt. ind.*) ; on high, 1649.

[lyche] (A.S. gelīc, *adj.*, also gelīca, *n.*, L. iliche, ilike, O. like), lych*e* evene, 10. — lyk*ẹ*, 1033, 1039, 1076 ; lyk*e*, 1124.

longe (A.S. lang, long, L. long, O. lang), Yf hit so longe tyme dure, 303 ; And oft I mused longe while, 1287 ; That bore hath vp longe while, 1484. — long*ẹ*, 251, 252, 381, 446, 1354.

[lovde] (A.S. hlūd), *only in* lovd*e* (lowd*e*), 767, 1958.

olde (A.S. eald, ald, L^a. æld, ald, alde, olde, L^b. hold, holde, O. ald), Of olde tyme(s), 1155. — olde (*l.* gold*ẹ*) werke, 127 ; old(e), 995 f, 2064 f (*both :* tolde *pp.*).

[swifte] (A.S. swift, O. swift), *no example*. — swift*ẹ*, 350.

[woode] (A.S. wōd), *no example*. — as thou were wod(e), 202 f (: bloode *n.*).

> Note 1. — The following list shows monosyllabic adjectives ending in Anglo-Saxon in a consonant which take no *-e* in H. F. It will be noted that *-e* is quite commonly written, but it is mute always.
>
> blak, 1647 ; blak(e), 1671 f (: take *2 sg. imp.*). — blynd(e), 1570 f (: wynde *n.*) ; blend*ẹ*, 681. — broun(e), 139 f (: dovne *adv.*). — cold*e*, 1163. — crips, 1386 f. — ded(e), 1876 f (: hede *n.*). — domb*e*, 656. — frerr*ẹ*, 647. — ful, 31, 1027, 1514, 1557, 1687, 1805, 1834, 1942, 1943, 2122. — hool, 1270. — leef, 1999. — lous*e*, 1286.

— lyght, 746, 1096. — red(e), 135 f (: hede *n.*), 1647 f (: lede *n.*). — ryght, 1614. — sad, 2089. — smal*e*, 487. — sooth*e*, 502, 2072 ; soth(e), 2051 f (: dothe *3 sg. pr. ind.*) ; sooth, 987. — strong(e), 1457 f (: endlonge *adv.*). — syk(e), 1270 (: magike *n.*). — war, 496, 1407, 1989. — whit*e*, 135, 938. — worth*e*, 727.

Note 2. — For dissyllables in the indefinite use, see the following : besy*e*, 1472. — blissfull, 518. — blody, 1239. — bret ful, 2123. — burned, 1387. — drery, 179. — englyssh, 1470. — golden, 1723. — grenyssh, 1647. — hevy, 738, 1440, 1473. — knowen, 1736. — lewed, 1096 f ; lewde (F B *corrupt*), 866. — liltyng, 1223. — lyghted, 769. — naked, 133. — rechcheles, 397. — sely, 513. — sory, 1790. — shrewde, 275, 1619. — stiryng, 478. — swartissh*e* (F B *swart*[*e*]), 1647. — tynned, 1482. — vncouth*e*, 1279. — wery, 115. — woful, 214. — wonder, 1082. — wonderful, 62. — worthy, 708, 1669. — yren, 1457. — ywel, 1786.

§ 50. The following adjectives of Germanic origin also show an *-e* in *H.F.*

bad [de] (A.S. bæddel ?), Though they goon in ful bad [de] lese, 1768. Such is the reading of Sk. and Wi., though T alone shows *-e*. We have a very good verse without *-e*.

wikke (cf. M.E. wicche, A.S. wicc(e)a 'wizard,' wicce 'witch'), that nas no thinge wikke, 1346 f (: thikke *adj.*). — wikkyd, 1620.

§ 51. Final unaccented *-e* in adjectives of Romance origin is preserved in *H.F.* (cf. Child, § 19 ; ten Brink, § 239).

I. digne (O.F. digne), 1426. — huge (O.F. ahuge), 1607. — Iust*e* (O.F. juste), 719. — large (O.F. large), 482, 1238, 1412, 1440 f (: charge *n.*) ; at hys large, 745 f (: charge *n.*). *But,* That hath a ful large whele to turne, 1450. In this verse, however, P C T have *largë* by omitting *a*. *Definite use,* 926. — nyce (O.F. nice), 276 f (: vice *n.*) ; nys*e*, 920 ; *definite use,* nyce, 287. — queynt [e] (O.F. cointe). Of the three instances of the use of this adjective, final *-e* is written but once — T 228. The lines are :

And queynt [e] maner of figures, 126 ;
Goynge in a queynt array, 228 ;
This queynt [e] hous about [e] went [e], 1925.

Final *-e* is not absolutely required, but it should doubtless be supplied.

II. Words in *-ble.*

agreable, 1097 f. — double, 285. — fauorable, 1479 f. — feble, 1132. — impossible, 702 ; impossib(il)le, 1334 f. — noble,

1416 ; *definite use*, 469, 1409, 1535.

> Note. — French *-é* is of course preserved, — pryuee, 767 ; *and* prevy, 285.

§ 52. Some Romance adjectives take an *-e* in *H.F.* that have none in Old French.

clere (O.F. cler), And hyt [is] cleped clere laude, 1575 ; cler*e*, 983 ; *but* cler(e), 1482 f (: pilere *n.*).
comune (O.F. comun), *only in* in comune, 1548 f (: fortune *n.*).
devyne (O.F. divin), *vocative*, devyne vertu, 1101.
femynyne (O.F. feminin), A femynyne creature, 1365.
fyne (O.F. fin). Final *-e* is regularly written, but it can hardly be sounded in any case : Arionis harp[e] fyn(e), 1005 f (delphyne *pr. n.*) ; yren fyn(e), 1431 f (: saturnyne *post. adj. sg.*) ; fyn*e*, 1348.
pure (O.F. pur), of pure kynde, 824 ; *definite use*, 280 (T *alone shows the line*.

> Note. — For examples of the singular number of Romance adjectives in the indefinite use, see the following :
> certèyn(e), 502 f (: seyne *pp.*) ; certeyn, 159\`. — confùse̦, 1517. — conseruatyf, 847. — cruell*e*, 1463. — curious(e), 29 f (: melancolyouse *pred. adj. sg.*). — desèrt*e*, 417. — devỳs, 917 f. — disèsperàt, 2015. — dyuers, 1574 ; dyvers, 1976. — encombrouse̦, 862. — ententyf, 1120. — eryd, 485. — famouse̦, 1338. — imperiall, 1361 f. — màliciouse̦, 93. — mèlancòlyoùs(e), 30 f (: curiouse *pred. adj. sg.*). — naturell, 28 ; naturel, 1266 f. — noyouse̦, 574. — obedient, 2022 f. — overt(e), 718 f (: aperte *adv.*). — ovndye̦, 1386. — parfit, 44. — poetical, 1095. — saturnyn(e), 1432 f (: fyne *post. adj. sg.*). — special, 68. — synguler, 310. — v̇nfamoùse̦, 1146.

§ 53. In the definite use (that is, when preceded by a possessive or demonstrative pronoun or by the definite article), monosyllabic adjectives take an inflectional *-e*. (Child, § 32 ; ten Brink, § 235).

I. Ordinals.

ther shal the thrid[de] be, 308 ; the thirdde companye, 1657 ; the thirdd*e* [whele], 795 ; the thrid (+ *vowel*), 2070. — the ferthe companye, 1690. — the fifte route, 1703. — the sext[e] companye, 1727. — [the sevënth route, 1771]. — the tenthe day, 63, 111.

II. Monosyllabic Superlatives.

This lytel last[e] boke, 1093. — at the laste, 496 f; atte laste, 955 f, 1407 f, 1676 f; at the laste, 1128; at the last he, 555; atte last hyt, 1726; atte last (+ *vowel*), 1320, 2155.

> Rhyme words. — caste *pt. sg. ind.* (496, 955, 1407), faste *adv.* (1676). —

the next[e] laure, 1107; this next[e] folke, 1775.

III. Miscellaneous.

hys blake trumpe, 1637, 1865; his blake Clarioun, 1801. — hir blynde sone, 138; hys blynde neviwe, 617. — the derke pyne, 1512. — the (F *lacks* the) Duche tonge, 1234. — this lusty and riche place, 1356. — the swynt[e] catte, 1783. — the faire white mone, 2116. — hir yonge sone, 177.

IV. Some examples are here given of the definite form of words which occasionally show an -*e* in forms not obviously definite (cf. § 49).

his fals[e] forswerynge, 153. — hir fair[e] toun, 432. — this foule trumpes soun, 1642; his foule trumpes ende, 1646. — hir grete peyne, 312; the grete soun, 1025; the grete swogh, 1031; thy grete myght, 1092; The grete god of loues name, 1489; The grete poete, 1499; the gret[e] wikkednesse, 1813; the gret Omere, 1466; oure gret ese, 1753. — thys lovde fare, 1065.

V. *ovne* (A.S. āgen) is found only in the definite use, — thyn ovne boke, 712; thyn ovne sworen brother, 2101; Our ovne gentil lady, 1311.

§ 54. Occasionally, however, -*e* is dropped in the definite form of monosyllabic adjectives. (Child, § 36; ten Brink, § 236.

your ryght honde, 322; my ryght honde, 1294. But this phrase was pretty certainly felt as a compound. These are the only instances observed in *H.F.* if we except *the seventh route* (1711), and in this latter case the proper form doubtless is *seventh*[*ë*].

§ 55. In vocative phrases monosyllabic adjectives appear in the definite form when they precede the noun (as in A.S. *lēofa Bēowulf*). (Child, § 34; ten Brink, § 235).

faire blissfull, 518. — my leue brother, 816. — O wikke Fame, 349.

In definite and vocative phrases in which the adjective follows the noun the usage in *H.F.* is varied.

(*a*) *Without* -*e*, the welkene longe and brod(e), 1601 f (: abode *3 sg. pt. ind.*); lady bright, 1693 f (: myght *n.*); (*b*) *with*

-e, lady leefe and dere, 1827 f (: here *inf.*); Josephus the olde, 1433 f (: tolde *3 sg. pt. ind.*); the sonnes sonne the rede, 941 f (: lede *inf.*); the wounde smerte, 374 f (: herte *n.*).

§ 56. For adjectives of more than one syllable which do not stand at the end of the verse, the following rule as to -*e* in the definite and vocative constructions may be inferred from the usage of *H.F.*

Of adjectives of more than one syllable those alone take -*e* which have a primary or secondary accent on the ultima and are followed by a word accented on the first syllable.

The special cases may be stated as follows :
I. Dissyllabic paroxytone adjectives take no -*e* when the following word is accented on the first syllable. The verse will not bear such an arrangement of accents as òòòòò.
Example: *my crewel deth.* (See others in § 57).
II. For the same reason dissyllabic oxytone adjectives take no -*e* when the following word is accented on the second syllable.
Example : *hys mỳghtỳ merite* (§ 58).
III. Trisyllabic proparoxytone adjectives (òòò) take -*e* unless the following word is accented on the second syllable.
Example : *the Tròianỳsshë bloode* (§ 59).
IV. But trisyllabic proparoxytone adjectives take no -*e* when the following word is accented on the second syllable. The verse will not bear such an arrangement of accents as òòòòòò.
For lack of a better example : *the wònder mòst was thỳs* (§ 60).
V. For the same reason trisyllabic paroxytone adjectives take no -*e* when the following word is accented on the first syllable.
Examples under I.–IV. follow (§§ 57–60).

Note 1. — There is in *H.F.* no adjective of more than three syllables in the definite use. For a few in the indefinite form, see § 52, n.
Note 2. — For the definite use of the singular of adjectives of more than one syllable at the end of the verse, cf. *the fayrest[e]* (T *alone shows the line*), 281 f (: lest[e] *3 sg. pt. subj.*); *Cupido the rechcheles*, 668 f (: causeles *adv.*).

§ 57. I. Dissyllabic paroxytone adjectives take no -*e* in the definite and vocative uses when the following word is accented on the first syllable. (Cf. Child, § 35 ; ten Brink, § 246).

(*a*) Cf. the plural superlative : the fynest stones, 1351.
(*b*) thyn ovne sworen brother, 2101.
(*c*) the heuenyssh melodye, 1395.
(*d*) the holy Roode, 57. — his kyndely enclynynge, 734. — his kyndely place, 842. — the melky weye, 937. — the myghty Muse, 1399.
(*e*) Romance and Latin adjectives :
the cruelle lyfe, 36. — my crewel deth, 323. — Our ovne gentil lady, 1311. — the Troian nacion, 207 ; the Troian Eneas, 217.

§ 58. II. Dissyllabic oxytone adjectives take no -*e* in the definite use when the following word is accented on the second syllable.
that latỳn Poète, 1483. — hys myghtỳ merìte, 2019.

§ 59. III. Trisyllabic proparoxytone adjectives (òoò) take -*e* in the definite and vocative uses, unless the following word is accented on the second syllable.
the Tròianỳsshë blòode, 201. — his kỳndelỳch[ë] stède, 829.

§ 60. IV. But trisyllabic proparoxytone adjectives take no -*e* when the following word is accented on the second syllable. The verse will not bear such an arrangement of accents as òoòooò.
the wònder mòst was thỳs, 2058.

§ 61. For the same reason trisyllabic paroxytone adjectives take no -*e* when the following word is accented on the first syllable. *No example.*

§ 62. The following are the only examples of the vocative of adjectives of more than one syllable :
crewèl Junoo, 198. — devỳnë vèrtu, 1101.— O wòful Dìdo, 318.

§ 63. The *Hous of Fame* shows a few well-defined traces of the French inflection of adjectives ; observe especially *seynt*, *seynt*[*e*] (Child, § 37 ; ten Brink, § 242).
seynt (*masculine*), Seynt Iùlyane, 1022 ; by sèynt Thomas, 1131 ; bè seynt Gỳle, 1183 ; seynt[e] (*feminine*), sèynt[e] Màry, 573 ; by sèynt[e] clàre, 1066. It is true that in these examples final -*e* is nowhere written, but the metre certainly

requires an additional syllable before the feminine nouns in 573, 1066. The identity of use — in oaths every example — and the different requirements of metre seem clearly to establish French inflection in this word. Cf. further *beau sir* (643), *bele Isawde* (1796). And see the vocative expression *devỳne vèrtu* (1101). Perhaps the *-e* of *femynyne* (1365) is due to an association of this sort. Observe also the list of French adjectives that have an inorganic *-e* (§ 52.).

For the French plural in *-s* (Child, § 43; ten Brink, § 243), see *the goddys celestials*, 460 f (: signals *n.*).

§ 64. Adjectives in the Comparative Degree usually end in H.F. in *-er*.

(*a*) fouler, 1638. — gretter, 1378. — wydder, 797.
(*b*) lenger (A.S. lengra), 1282; lengere, 1371.
(*c*) better (A.S. bet(e)ra, bettra), 1667. — bet, — I am no bet, 108.
more (A.S. māra), I. as *adj. sing. indef.* with nouns and pronouns, — hit semed moche more, 500 f (: sore *inf.*); more Iolytee, 682; No more semed than a prikke, 907; welmore than hit was, 1290; waxen . . . more . . . Than hyt was, 1495; mor*e* encres, 2074; mor*e*, *20, 2082. — The A.S. þȳ-construction, — the more parte, 336, 344, 1881. II. more, *substantive use*, — what wilt thou more, 883 f (: sore *inf.*); What shulde I more telle, 1513; gan . . . to eche (*addere*) . . . more, 2067.
mo, moo, *plural* (A.S. mā, *neut. subs.*), 121, 123, 124, 125, 674, 675, 677, 679, 685 (*bis*), 686 (*bis*), 687, 689, 693, 695, 697, 1254, 1949 f (: goo *inf.*). Willert's emendation in the following verse seems very reasonable: And eke moo holdynge[s] in honde(s), 692.
wors[e] (A.S. wiersa, wyrsa), wors[e] name, 1620.

§ 65. The Comparative and Superlative of adjectives are sometimes formed by means of *more* and *most* (Child, § 38, *d*; cf. ten Brink, § 245).

A single example of each of these formations appears in H.F. — more clere entendement, 983. — most conseruatyf, 847.

§ 66. The Superlative of adjectives ends in *-est*.

leuest, — That hem were leuest, 87. — For *first*, see 145, 2097. For superlative in the definite use, cf. §§ 53, 56, 57, 70.

§ 67. The Plural of monosyllabic adjectives ends in -*e*.

In the following list no definite or vocative forms are included without notice. Here also are included adjectives which sometimes or always have -*e* in the singular.

I. Adjectives standing immediately before the nouns modified :

faire (A.S. fæger ; for *sing*. cf. § 49), *1967.

goode (A.S. gōd ; for *sing*. cf. § 49). But we have no certain instance of sounded -*e* for this word. It occurs only in the expression *good werkes*, variously written by the several authorities. We may fairly assume that B T are correct in writing *werke* (*sing*.) in 1558 :

Of good werke yive vs good renoun.

In 1666 all (except T, which omits *now*) read :

That now your good werkes be wiste. In this case we should doubtless have *good*[*e*].

P C T are certainly correct in 1707 :

To hide (F B *And hidden*) her gode werkes eke. This is better suited both to sound and sense.

But there is no question of lack of final -*e* here :

Good werkes shal you noght availle, 1616. (Cf. § 68).

grete (A.S. grēat ; for *sing*. cf. § 49), 53, 900, 902, 1154, 1192.

lowde (A.S. hlūd ; for *sing*. cf. § 49), 1217.

newe (A.S. nēowe, nīowe ; for *sing*. cf. § 46), 654, 1886, 1887.

olde (A.S. eald, ald ; for *sing*. cf. § 49), 694, 1442. But in neither case is -*e* sounded. The verses :

Of olde forleten aqueyntaunces, 694 ;

As wel as other olde mervaylles, 1442.

But in the latter example P C T give a verse without *olde :*

As wel as of other meruayles. (Cf. § 68).

ryche (A.S. rīce), 123, 1322.

slowe (A.S. slāw), 1778.

smale (A.S. smæl), 1209.

II. Adjectives following the nouns they modify :

falwe (A.S. fealu, fealo), 1936.

ful (A.S. full. *Sing*. ful), (+ *vowel*), 1396, 1778.

glade (A.S. glæd), 1889 f (: made *3 sg. pt. ind*.

grene (A.S. grēne grǣne ; for *sing*. cf. § 49), 1937.

lyght[e] (A.S. leoht, liht, *shortened from* lēoht. *Sing*. lyght), 743 f (: hight[e] *n*.). But -*e* is written in none of the authorities.

ofte (A.S. oft, *adv*.), 35 f (: Vn-softe *adj. post. sg.*).

olde (A.S. eald, ald ; for *sing*. cf. § 49), 1233.

rede (A.S. rēad. *Sing*. rede), 1936 f (: rede *1 sg. pr. ind.*).

yonge (A.S. geong, etc.), 1233 f (: tonge *n*.).

III. fele (A.S. feola, fela, Ps. N. feolu, feolo ; really old neut. adj.), names fele, 1137 f (: wele *n.*) ; fel*e* yen, 1381 ; fel*e* vpstondyng eres, 1389 ; entrees As fel*e*, 1946.
fewe (A.S. fēawe, fēawa, Ps. fēa), they were wonder fewe, 1691 f (: in a rewe).
IV. The single example of a monosyllabic superlative in the plural appears without *-e :* Where thou maist most tydynges here, 2025.
V. Cardinal numerals (Child, § 39, *c* ; ten Brink, § 247).
foure (A.S. fēower, North. feuer, fēor), the bestes foure, 1383 f (: honoure *inf.*).
sevene (A.S. seofoṅ, W.S. seofan, seofen, siofon), Doughtres sevene, 1007 f ; sterres sevene, 1376 f ; other seuene, 1437 f.
  Rhyme words. — heuene, (1007, 1376), neuene *inf.* (1437).
eighte (A.S. eahta, North æhta, æhto, æhtowe), hir eighte sustren, 1401.
twelue (A.S. twelf, North. twœlf), Many thousand tymes twelue, 1216 f, 2126 f (*both :* hem selue).
  Note. — Other numerals, — *on*, *oon* (see § 79), *two* (116 f, 299 f, 689, 1144 f, 2093, 2104), *twoo* (772), *three* (204), *XX*ᵗⁱ. (1335, 2119), *sixty* (1979), *thousand* (1216, 1949, 2119, 2126), *thousandẹ* (75, 1495).
VI. Monosyllabic participles (see also § 68).
An how his shippes dreynte were, 233 ; Thilke that vnbrende were, 173 ; Been al the dores .... vnshet[te], 1953 f (: let *impedire.*).
VII. Romance adjectives :
noble (O.F. noble), noble gestes, 1737. — pore (O.F. povre), por*e* and ryche, 1532.
VIII. Adjectives which are both plural and definite of course have *-e :*
the Egles fethres bright[e] (F B *lack the line*), 507 f (: lyght *inf.*) ; the fynest stones faire, 1351 f (: lapidaire *n.*) ; fals[e] theves (*vocative*), 1779 ;
  And with hys grym[me] pawes stronge
  Within hys sharpe nayles longe, 541-2 ;
the roches holowe, 1035 f (: swalowe *inf.*) ; hys shuldres hye, 1435 (: Iewerye *n.*) ; the olde gestes, 1515 ; my sorwes smert[e], 316 f (: hert *n.*) ; the dores wide, 1420 f (syde *n.*). — these straunge thynges, 1236.

§ 68. Monosyllabic perfect participles standing in the predicate regularly take no *-e* in the plural.
  (i.) Before consonants and at the end of the verse : — loues ... That ben (FB *lack* ben) betydẹ, 680 ; in the see were

lefte behynde, 238 ; we ben wel quyt, 1614 f (: hyt *pro.*) ;
your good werkes be wist(e), 1666 f (: leste *3 sg. pr. ind.*) ;
corovnes wroght ful of losynges, 1317. — (ii.) Before vowels
and *h :* — his shippes . . . were . . . lost he nyste where,
234 ; youre Actes red and songe, 347 ; They wer set as thik,
1350.

But in three cases the *-e* appears : And how his shippes
dreynte were, 233 ; Thilke that vnbrende were, 173 ; Been al
the dores . . . vnshet[te], 1953 f (: let *inf.*). In the last
example F alone shows the abbreviated forms *vnshet, let.*

§ 69. Monosyllabic adjectives standing in the predicate do not
always take *-e* in the plural (Child, § 41 ; ten Brink, § 234).

let your werkes be ded(e), 1701 f (: hede *n.*) ; ye (*vos*) be lyke
the swynt[e] catte, 1783 ; be ye (*vos*) wood(e), 1713 f
(: goode *n. acc.*) ; they were wod(e), 1809 f (: hode *n.*).

So occasionally when the plural adjective is used attribu-
tively.

Ten Brink's remark, " Im Plural des attributiv stehenden
Adjectivs (gleichviel ob starker oder schwacher Flexion) tritt
die Apocope [des flexivischen *-e*] kaum ein ; niemals, wenn
der Adjectiv voransteht " (§ 236), is expressly contradicted
by the following verse :

Of olde forleten aqueyntaunces, 694. So also :

As wel as other olde mervayles, 1442. In the latter
verse, however, P C T show variant readings, omitting *olde.*
To these we may add :

Good werkes shal you noght availle, 1616. But *good
werkes* is a quasi-compound.

> Note. — For plurals standing before vowels, cf. fressh (1156),
> goode (1756), good (1780), ryche (1532), wise (1756). For
> other examples of plurals in the predicate, cf. glade (645 f),
> grene (1947), meke (1402 f), white (1937 f), wide (1952 f),
> wrothe (2103 f), y-lyche (1328 f).

§ 70. For adjectives of more than one syllable which do not
stand at the end of the verse, the rule as to *-e* in the plural
is the same as that already stated for the definite and vocative constructions (§ 56). Of such adjectives those alone
take *-e* which have a primary or secondary accent on the
ultima, and are followed by a word accented on the first syllable (cf. Child § 40 ; ten Brink, § 233).

(*a*) They wer a-cheked bothe two, 2093 ; arryved were, 1047 ;

somme corouned wer, 1316; boystes Crammed ful, 2129; shrippes entremedled with, 2124; feyned reparacions, 688; for-leten aqueyntaunces, 694; greses growen in, 1351; dores opened wide, 1952; roten slowe techches, 1778; we be served, 337; longe y-served loues, 678; they .... Shul thus be shamed, 1634; wenyed wondres, 2118.
(b) we wrechched wymmen, 335; wikked thewes, 1834.
(c) vs ... happy vnto, 1757; ye maisty Swyne, 1777; myghty werkes, 1504; his slepy thousande sones, 75; sondry glees, 1252; sondry habitacles, 1194; sondry regiouns, 1529; sondry stages, 122; these sory creatures, 1632; thy werray neygh[e]bor[e]s, 649; seuene ... worthy for to neuene, 1438; vs ... worthy wise and gode, 1756.
(d) These ben eyryssh bestes, 932; the ayerissh bestes, 965.
(e) fele vpstondyng eres, 1389; wonder thynges, 674, 1893; ydel al oure lyfe y-be, 1733; ye ydel wrechches, 1777.
(f) certeyn ascendentes, 1268; dyvers transmutacions, 1969; famouse folkes names, 1137; famous were, 1249; the merveloùse signàls, 459; So pàlpablè they shùlden be, 869; many subtile compassinges, 1188.

§ 71. The treatment of the plural of adjectives of more than one syllable at the end of the verse is illustrated by the following examples:

 Be we cried or still y-rovned
 Thus saugh I fals and sothe compovned, 2107–8;
we ben deceyuyd (F *lacks the line*), 340 f (: receyved *pp.*).
 For the single instance of the French plural (Child, § 43), cf. *the goddys celestials*, 460 f (: signals *n.*).

§ 72. Adjectives in A.S. -*līc* (-*lic*), O.N. -*ligr*, appear in *H.F.* with the ending -*ly*.

Ten Brink's theory (§ 270) that Chaucer was inclined to use -*lich* instead of -*ly* when the following word began with a vowel is not supported in *H.F.* There is but a single example of -*lich*, as follows:

Hath his kyndelych[e] stede, 829. Here *lych*[*e*] is certainly correct, and appears to be used solely to fill out the measure of the verse. The variants are, — B *kyndly*, T *kyndlyche*, PC *lack the verse*.
frendly chere, 1743; frendlỳ manere, 278; euery kyndely thynge, 730; a kyndely stede, 731; hys kyndely enclynynge, 734; his kyndely place, 842.

PRONOUNS.

§ 73. I. Personal Pronouns.

I (A.S. ic), 12, 13, 14, 52, 59, 61, 62, 64, 65, etc., etc. ; y, 477, 548, 764, 782, 850, 854, 864, etc. *I* is the ruling form.

 Rhyme words. — Adverbs in *-ly* (13, 52, 62, 129, 313, 582, 1046, 1128, 1320, 1391, 1404, 2138), why (999), mercy (1873), by (1989).

thou (A.S. þū), 202, 574, 577, 602, 603, 607, 615, 624, etc., etc. ; thow, 596, 793, 1839, etc. The reduced form *-ow* is very often attached to verbs, — artow, 1872 ; herestow, 1031, 1862 ; maistow, 1024 ; nostow, 1010 ; shaltow, 2026 ; wostow, 1000, 1784, 1791 ; *but*, — darst thou, 560 ; fairest thou, 887 ; mayste thou, 747 ; mayst thou, 826 ; shalt thou, 711 ; wilt thou, 883 ; wost thou, 781, 790, 863. The contracted form is uniform in B, while P never shows it.

 Rhyme word. — now (778).

he (A.S. hē), 14, 78, 81, 98, 101, 102, 107, 115, 166 (*bis*), 176, 185, 187, etc., etc. ; hee, 454, 904, etc. ; hye, 1595. Common in rhyme, — 193, 225, 307, 364, 454, 904, etc.

she, 163, 184, 191, 235, 240, 268, 284, 296, 299, 300, etc., etc. ; shee, 256. Common in rhyme, — 242, 256, 323, 358, 1081, etc.

hyt, hit (A.S. hit), *nom., acc., and with prepositions*, 2, 6, 46, 50, 51, 83, 91, 92, 97, 102, 112, 130, and *passim ; occasionally* yt, it, 822, 1033, 1042, 1108, 1623, 1680. In rhyme there are two examples, — hyt(te), 701 f (: witte *n.*) ; hyt, 1613 f (: quyt *pp. pred. plur.*). Except in our MS. *it* is the prevailing form.

me (A.S. mē), *dat., acc., and with prepositions.* (*a*) Dative without preposition, 119, 300, 313, 499, 560, 853, 870, etc. (*b*) Other oblique uses, 60, 107, 317 (mee), 324, 565, 576, and *passim.* Reflexive, 246, 1286. Common in rhyme, — 107, 324, 565, 576, 874, 887, 893, etc.

the (A.S. þē), *dat., acc., and with prepositions.* (*a*) Dative without preposition, 578, 601, 726, 782, 871, 894, etc. (*b*) Other oblique uses, 526, 598, 599, 600, 613, 627, 662, and *passim.* Reflexive, 627. Common in rhyme, 606, 648 (thee), 839, 870, 894, 1044, etc.

hym, him (A.S. him), *dat., acc., and with prepositions.* (*a*) Dative without preposition, 32, 101, 255, 423, etc.

(*b*) Other oblique uses, 169, 191, 257, 259, 260, 412, 413, 420, and *passim*. Reflexive, 231, 389, etc. Not in rhyme.

hir, her (A.S. hire), *dat., acc., and with prepositions*. (*a*) Dative without preposition, 263, 368, 395, etc. (*b*) Other oblique uses, 185, 232, 267, 294, 295, 297, 298, 371, 403, 414, 416, 418, 424, etc. Within the verse final -*e* is nowhere written, and this is true of the other MSS. as well. In rhyme there are two examples, both with sounded -*e*, — to hire, 420 f (: swere *inf.*) ; here, *acc.*, 1003 f (bere *n.*).

we (A.S. wē), 337, 339, 886, 1553, 1697 f (: bounte *n.*), etc.

ye (A.S. gē), 330, 338, 343, 512, 520, and *passim* ; *as singular*, 213, 320, 322, 326, and *passim*.

 Rhyme words. — pitee *n.* (326), be *inf.* (1258).

they (O.N. þeir), 84, 683, 706, 744, 869, 999, and *passim*. Does not occur in rhyme.

vs (A.S. ūs), *dat., acc., and with prepositions*. (*a*) Dative without preposition, 1, 58, 406, 1536, 1609, 1748, etc. (*b*) Other oblique uses, 293, 465, 466, 470, 1313, 1537, etc. Reflexive, 2102.

 Rhyme words. — Theseus (406), Venus (465), thus (470), Eolus (1862).

yow (A.S. ēow), *dat., acc., and with prepositions*. (*a*) Dative without preposition, 65, 109, 150, 529, 547, etc. ; yow(e), 1418 f, 1822 f. (*b*) Other oblique uses, 252, 339, 1179, 1256, 1343, and *passim*. (*c*) As singular, 324, 329 (yow*e*), 346, and often.

 Rhyme words. — how (547), nowe (1418, 1822).

hem, hym, him (A.S. him, heom), *dat., acc., and with prepositions*. (*a*) Dative without preposition, 40, 83, 87, 90, 684, etc. (*b*) Other oblique uses, 15, 19, 22, 88, 474, 640, 928 (P *them*), and *passim*. hym, 1210, 1211, 1212, 1214. him 1582.

§ 74. II. Possessive Pronouns.

my, myn (A.S. mīn). I. Singular. (*a*) my *before consonants :* my gynnynge, 66 ; my sweuene, 79 ; my fauor, 519 ; my brayn, 525 ; my dreme, 527 ; my felynge, 552 ; my name, 558 ; my mynde, 564 ; my ryght honde, 1294 ; *also* 583, 702, 710, 776, 871, 1182, etc., etc. (*b*) myn *before vowels :* myn ye, 498, 906, 1492 ; myn ymagynacion, 728 ; myn age, 1986 ; myn egle, 1990 ; myn entente, 2000 ; myn entent, 2132 ; *but* my arte, 1882. (*c*) myn *before h :* myn hede, 273, 1103, 1702 ; myn hert, 1148 ; *but* my hert (P *myn*), 1570. (*d*) myn *postpositive :* lady myn he seyde. II. Plural. (*a*) my : my fete, 1050. (*b*) myn : myn eyen, 495, 1408. III. myn *noun omitted :* Ywel thrifte come to your Iowes And eke to myn, 1787.

thy, thyn (A.S. þīn). I. Singular. (*a*) thy *before consonants :* thy prowe, 579 ; thy frende, 582 ; thy trouthe, 613, 889 ; thy witte, 620 ; thy studye, 633 ; thy labour, 652 ; thy grete myght, 1092 ; *also* 658, 925, 971, 1405, 1537, etc., etc. (*b*) thyn *before vowels :* thyn engyne, 528 ; thyn abstynence, 660 ; thyn advertence, 709 ; thyn ovne boke, 712 ; thyn ye, 935 ; thyn auenture, 1052 ; thyn other trumpe, 1672 ; thyn ovne sworen brother, 2101. (*c*) thyn, thy, *before h :* thyn hede, 632 ; thyn hande, 741 ; thyn heuynesse, 2011 ; thy hede (P *thyn*), 621 ; thy house (P *thyn*), 659 ; thy hertys reste, 2017. II. Plural. (*a*) thy : thy werray neyghbors, 649 ; thy dors, 650. (*b*) thyn : thyn eres, 879.

hys, his (A.S. his), so *passim* with both masculine and neuter nouns singular and plural : his slepy thousand sones, 75 ; his fals forswerynge, 153 ; his chere and his lesynge, 154 ; hys bakke, 169 ; hys honde, 171 ; his shippes, 233 ; his ye, 291 ; his aventure, 463 ; hys grym pawes, 541 ; hys sharpe nayles, 542 ; hys arte, 627 ; his other clarioun, 1579, etc., etc. The spelling *hys* is the commoner of the two.

hir, her, hyr (A.S. hire), so *passim* before vowels and consonants singular and plural : hir figure, 132 ; hir hede, 134 ; hyr hede, 136 ; hir dowves, 137 ; hir blynde sone, 138 ; Hyr lyfe hir loue hir luste hir lorde, 258 ; hir hondes two, 299 ; her skyn, 1229 ; hir fete, 1374, 1391 ; hir eyen, 1379 ; hir heere, 1386 ; hir eighte sustren, 1401, etc., etc. The form *hir* largely predominates, *hyr*, *her* being very unusual except in CT.

oure, our (A.S. ūre). I. Singular. (*a*) *before consonants :* our myght, 1694 ; our name, 1696 ; oure lyfe, 1733 ; oure gret ese, 1753 ; oure fame, 1836. (*b*) *before vowels* : our ovne gentil lady, 1311. (*c*) *before h* : oure herte, 1749. II. Plural. (*a*) oure sorwes, 1610 ; our werkes, 1696.

your (A.S. ēower), so *passim*. In the examples cited below singular antecedents are marked as such. I. Singular : Your loue ne your bonde (*s.*), 321 ; your ryght honde (*s.*), 322 ; your loue, 341 ; your cause (*s.*), 1563 ; your soule (*s.*), 1612 ; your askynge, 1700. II. Plural : your good werkes, 1666 ; your werkes, 1701.

her, hir (A.S. heora, hiera), so *passim*. I. Singular. (*a*) *before consonants* : hir signifiaunce, 17 ; her brayne, 24 ; her thought, 92 ; hir matere, 637 ; her description, 987 ; hir fame, 1146; her tyme, 1249, 1523, etc., etc. (*b*) *before vowel*: her axyng, 1541. (*c*) *before h*: her hert, 1799; her hode, 1810. II. Plural. (*a*) her loues, 86; hir kyndes, 968; her places, 1014; her fames, 1139; her loses, 1688; her goode werkes, 1707; her lestes, 1738, etc. The spelling *her* predominates largely. P shows *here* frequently, always monosyllabic. C has *theyr* occasionally, — 156, 987, etc.

§ 75. III. Reflexive and Intensive Pronouns.

The compounds of *self* (A.S. self, sylf, etc.) appear in *H.F.* in the forms -*self*, -*selfe*, -*selue*, -*selfen* (Child, § 46; ten Brink, § 255. Cf. also § 79, below).

my selfë. — I wil my selfë alle hyt drynke, 1880.

thy selfe, thy selfen. — Thow demest of thy selfe amys, 596; And wost thy selfen outtirly Disesperat of alle blys, 2014–15.

hym self[ë], hym selfe. — And alle the batayles that hee Was at hym selfe and eke hys knyghtis, 454–5; Euery sercle causynge other Wydder than hym self[ë] was, 796–7.

hir selfe, hir selfë, hir selfe. — Wherfore she slowe hir selfe allas, 268; Quod she to hir-selfë thoo, 319; She rofe hir selfë to the herte, 373; She henge hir selfe ryght be the hals, 394.

hem selue. — A fer fro hem alle be hem selue, 1215 f (: twelue *num.*).

§ 76. IV. Demonstrative Pronouns.

No distinction is attempted between the substantive and adjective uses.

that (A.S, þæt), 7, 9, 20, 244, 563, 651, 951, 1064, etc., etc.; *in rhyme*, 1887 f, 2050 f (*both :* what *pro.*).

thoo, tho (A.S. þā), Of thoo that hadde large fame, 1412; Tho behynde (be)gunne vp lepe, 2150.

thilke, *plur.*, Thilke that vnbrende were, 173.

that ylke, *sing.*, that ylke place, 1169; that ylke shrewe, 1842.

this, thys. I. *Sing.*, 8, 9, 11, 20, 23, 53, 54, 74, 157, 239, 279, 286, and *passim*. Common in rhyme, — 517, 577, 652, 699, 729, 863, 914, etc. There is one instance of *these :* Of these yates florisshinges, 1301, — apparently through misapprehension of the number of *yates*. II. *Plur.* these (thise, thes), *monosyllabic except in* 2009: Fynally with these thinges. *Cf.* these, 11, 12, 37, 716, 750, 845, 1008, 1264, 1288, 1331, 1455, 1471, 1503, 1632, 1793, 1894, 1938, 1939, 2127; thise, 1225; thes fumiygaciones, 1264.

thys ylke, this ilke, *sing.*, thys ylke noble quene, 1409; this ilke noble quene, 1535. — these ilke, *plur.*, Which these ilke louers leden, 37.

Note. — A remnant of the A.S. demonstrative þǣm, þām, þān, is seen in the phrases *for the nones* (2087) and *wyth the nones* (2099 f). The A.S. instrumental appears in *the ferther* . . . *the gretter* (1651–2), and in such phrases as *the lesse* (620).

§ 77. V. Interrogative Pronouns.

whoo, *nom.* (A.S. hwā), 474.
whos, *gen.*, not observed.
whom, *dat. and acc.*, not observed.
what, I. Subs., *nom.*, 601, 1147, 1158, 1839, etc.; *acc.*, 320, 1636, 1784 f (what(te)), 1887 f, 2094 f, etc. II. Adj., *nom.*, 781, 1123, 1342, 1543, etc.; *acc.*, 475, 587, etc.; of what congeled matere, 1126.
> Rhyme words. — catte *n.* (1784), that *pro.* (1887, 2094).
> Note. — For *what = why* cf. 1282, 1513. Remnants of the instrumental *hwȳ* are seen in *why* (995, 1000 f) and in *fforwhȳ* (20), *for whȳ* (725), *for whı̄* (1183).

which, see under Relatives, § 78.

§ 78. VI. Relative Pronouns and Pronominal Adjectives, and the Interrogative (etc.) *which*.

that, *a general relative for all genders and numbers*, 38, 54, 70, 71, 72, 77, 81, 82, 83, 84, 87, 90, 91, and *passim*; that = *id quod*, 354; 361, 1024, 1519; also what that = *id quod*, 110, 380, etc.; that = *ei qui*, 1550; that . . . his = whose, 139; that . . . her = whose, 1402.
whom, — For whom was maked moch compleynt, 924; *also* Of whom that speketh virgilius, 1244.
who-so, who so, *12, 94, 447, 807, etc.; who-sò, 377.
what so, — what so cometh fro any tonge, 721; *also* what so euer in al these three Is spoken, 716–17.
what, as a "general relative," — in what place That hem were leuest for to stonde, 87–88; For what I drye or what I thynke I wil my selfe alle hyt drynke, 1879–80.
> Interesting are, — What with his sours and with my drede, 551; The thynges that I herde there What a lovde and what in ere, 2057–8.

which. — I. Interrogative (in indirect questions and exclamations): which (= *quales*) they ben, 999; which (= *qualis*) a congregacion, 2034. II. Relative. (i.) Sing. (*a*) *pronoun:* which, 446, 607, 755, 843, etc.; whiche, 529, 969, 1493, 1581, etc.; whiche, 37, 1349, 1444, etc.; which that, 176, 437, 531, 633, etc.; wich that, 1077; whiche that, 609, 949, 1326, 2156. (*b*) *adjective:* thurgh which magike, 1269; vnto whichẹ place, 733. (ii.) Plur. (*a*) which 772, 1265, etc.; whichẹ, 1255, 1427, 1455; which that, 931, 1253, etc. the whichẹ, the which, — *only in singular*. *Pronoun*, the which as, 64; the whichẹ, 1069. *Adjective*, the whichẹ Anchises, 171.

suchẹ (A.S. swilc, swelc). I. Sing., *always monosyllabic*: suchẹ a, 103, 517, 1524, 1645, 1841; suchẹ another, 1296, 1367, 1914; swich a nother, 1171; suchẹ vntrouthe, 384, 395; suchẹ folk (F *folkes*), 1828; suchẹ noblesse, 471; suchẹ richesse, 472; suchẹ renoun, 1709, etc. — he suchẹ semed, 264; Suchẹ as, 1746; That oure fame suchẹ be knowe, 1836. II. Plur., *dissyllabic*: suchẹ dremes, 35; suchẹ wordes, 311; suchẹ thynges, 1889. But in the following verse *suchë* gives a harsh reading: But these be no suchẹ tydynges, 1894.

§ 79. VII. Other pronominal words.

samë (O.N. samr; *definite* sami; cf. A.S. same, *adv.*), the same, *pro. sg.*, 2063. Adjective *in the definite use*: the same wyse, 1061; the same wight, 1076; the same body, 1081; the same thing the same bone, 1774.

selfë (A.S. sylf, self; *definite*, sylfa, selfa), the selfe day, 1157.

sommẹ, somẹ, sum (A.S. sum), *monosyllabic except in rhyme*. I. Adj. (*a*) *sing.*: sommẹ man, 29; sommẹ disport, 664; sommẹ recompensacion, 665; sommẹ maner thinge, 670; sommẹ good, 1998, etc.; sum place, 827. (*b*) *plur.*: sommẹ newe tydynges, 1886. II. Subs., *plur.*: sommẹ, 1539; somẹ, 1540; sommẹ, 6, 34, 1538; sommẹ, 5 f (: come *inf.*); al and some, 46 f (: come *inf.*).

sumwhat, sommẹ what (A.S. sumhwæt), sumwhat here, 1998; sommẹ what for to eche, 2065. Also used adverbially, — sumwhat agreable, 1097.

other (A.S. ōðer). I. Adj. (*a*) *sing.*: other thinge, 891; other maner, 1219; that other syde, 1151; non other auttor, 314; another booke, 657; another whele, 794; another ayre, 813, etc. (*b*) *plur.*: other werkes, 54; noon other weyes, 585; other thynges, 643, 743; other clerkys, 760; other seuene, 1437, etc. II. Subs. (*a*) *sing.*: another, 307, 1296; a nother, 1171; other, 796 f, 799, 815 f, 817, 2102 f. (*b*) *plur.*: other, 23, 1246, 2151.

Rhyme word. — brother *n*.

Note. — For the *gen. sing.*, cf. otheres sterynge, 800; others ere, 2044. Perhaps the *gen. pl.* is seen in *other heles*, 2153.

echẹ, ech (A.S. ǣlc), *adj.*, echẹ disese, 89; *subs.*, echẹ of hem, 745, 2096; ech of the pynnacles, 1193; echẹ of these, 1470;

eche of vs, 1537 ; They had good fame eche deserued, 1545 ; eche with other, 2102 ; she gan yeve eche hys name, 2112. — echon, 150 f (: anon).

euery (A.S. æfre + A.S. ælc) counts as a dissyllable (cf. ten Brink, § 262). The usual spelling is *euery* (1, 58, 65, 80, 99, 210, 254, etc., etc.) ; but also *euerych* (817), and *eueryche* (47, 975).

euerychon, euerychoon, 337 f, 1660 f, 1717 f, 1772 f, 1776 f.
> Rhyme words. — anon (1660, 1717, 1772), groon *inf.* (337), doon *pp.* (1776).

any, eny (A.S. ænig), *sing.* and *plur.*, — usually spelt *any* (99, 261, 333, 478, etc.) ; but also *eny* (1074, 1122).

eyther (A.S. ægðer), *adj.*, on eyther syde, 1419 ; eyther bere, 1004.

neyther (A.S. ne + A.S. ægðer), *subs.*, neyther of hem, 2094.

bothe (O.N. báðir), *adj.*, Til hyt at bothë brinkes bee 803 ; They wer a-cheked bothë two, 2093 ; bothë, *subs.*, 2104 f (: wrothe *pred. adj. pl.*).

ovne, see § 53, V.

men = one. The use of *men* as an indefinite pronoun (= Ger. *man*) is very common. The verb accompanying it seems sometimes singular, sometimes plural ; and it is often difficult to distinguish between this indefinite *men* and *men* meaning people in general : — men clepeth, 73, 937 ; men may . . . rede, 385 ; men may casten, 1048 ; men seyn, 1147 ; men had writen, 1156 ; men myght hyt han herd, 1929 ; men may yet seen, 1948 ; etc. The shortened form *me* occurs once, — B 73. Observe also : As smale as *man* may se, 487.

oon, oo, o ; noon, non, no (A.S. ān, nān). I. The full forms are found in all substantive constructions ; so also in adjective constructions when the adjective follows its noun or stands by itself in the predicate. Thus, — That useth oon, 562 ; Hier stant ther non, 1117 ; oon or two, 1144 ; oon seyde, 1477 ; good fame non, 1560 f ; that oon, 1855 f; oon that stoode, 1869 ; porter ther is noon, 1954 ; oon had herde, 2060. II. In the attributive position, *oo*, *o* are regular before consonants, *oon* occurring once ; *no* is the invariable form before consonants, *noon*, *non* before vowels and *h*. — o thynge, 1068 ; o sentence, 1100 ; oo thing, 1650 ; *but* oon thyng, 2002 ; oo tydynge, 2109. — no man, 32, 60, 680, 763 ; no maner creature, 489 ; no wonder, 913 ; no fors, 999, 1011, 1910 ; no richesse, 1423 ; no fame, 1709, 1716 ; no good, 1795 ; etc. — noon oppinion, 55 ; non other auttour, 314 ;

noon arte, 335 ; noon harme, 577 ; non harme, 1045. *Plural.*
(*a*) no tydynges, 644 ; (*b*) noon other weyes, 585.

ought, aught (A.S. āwiht, āht, ōwiht, ōht), whan thou hast of ought knowynge, 891 ; Wilt thou lere of sterres aught, 993 f ; ought thow knowest, 912 (F B *lack the line*).

noght, naught, novght (A.S. nāwiht, etc.), of noght elles, 646 ; Sovne is noght but eyre, 765 ; quod y ryght naught, 994 f ; Good werkes shal yow noght availle, 1616 ; Ne of Fame wolde they novght, 1712 f ; Ne elles noght from wymmen sent, 1742 ; *also* That skorne hyt noght(e), 91 f ; goo noght awey, 317 ; And noght hym nor his folke dispisest, 638 ; noght only, 647 ; Hyt nedeth noght, 1072, 1299 ; Though I hem noght be ordre telle, 1453 ; me lyst hyt noght, 1797 ; etc.

many a (A.S. manig), *sing.*, *dissyllabic*, — many a shrewde vice, 275 ; many a rowe, 448 ; many a citezeyn, 930 ; many a creature, 2040 ; many a peler, 1421. — many oon (*trisyl.*), 760 f (: platon *pr. n.*), 1207 f (: glascurion *pr. n.*), 1308 f (: anoon), 1915 f (: goon *inf.*) ; *but* many oon (*dissyl.*), 2026. — many, *plur.*, many wyse, 771 ; many subtile compassinges, 1188 ; many thousand tymes twelue, 1216 ; many frenges, 1318 ; many other werkynges, 1944 ; *subs.*, So many formed be nature, 2039.

§ 80. *Al*, singular.

I. In its strictly adjective use *al* is commonest before the definite article and other more or less definite words. Thus, — before *the*, 167, 201, 207, 259, 375, 451, 486, 906, 969, 988, 1114, 1181, 1525, 1601, 1629, 1633, 1640, 1684, 1807, 1826, 1829, 1932, 2055 ; before *this*, 348, 468, 1065, 1113, 1161, 1266, 1285, 1551, 1935 ; before *that*, 933, 1064 ; before *my*, 527, 552, 1016, 1175, 1986, 2023, 2132 ; before *thy*, 200, 2017 ; before *his*, 174, 428, 463, 611 ; before *hir* (*poss. sing.*), 362 (*bis*), 462 ; before *our*, 1694, 1733 ; before *your*, 1700 ; before *her* (*poss. plur.*), 156. — There are two examples before the indefinite article, — al a Realme, 704 ; all*e* a Citee, 2080. — In one expression only does it seem to qualify the noun immediately, — *al day* (386, 737). For *al dispence* (260) read *al the dispence* for metrical reasons. — For *alt his*, cf. 705, 1341, etc.

Note. — In these uses *al* is the prevailing spelling ; but *alle* (*monosyl.*) is not infrequent (201, 988, 1161, 1175, 1181, etc.) and *all* occurs rarely (933, 969).

II. As a substantive, *alle* (*monosyl.*) is the usual form ; but *al* occurs with some frequency, and there is an occasional *all*.

Examples : he that mouer ys of all(e), 81 f (: shalle *3 sg. pr. ind.*) ; send hem alle that may hem plese, 90 ; hyt had al be so, 262 ; alle that euer he myght swere, 422 ; al that I mette, 523 ; in hir matere al devisest, 637 ; alle that y of spake, 978 ; alle ys wele, 1021 ; Alle was of ston, 1184 ; alle that longeth vnto fame, 1200 ; flore and roof and all(e), 1344 f (: walle *n. nom.*) ; I wil my selfe alle hyt drynke, 1880 ; Alle mote oute, 2139. Here may also be put such uses as, — *when thy labour doon al ys* (652), *The halle was al ful* (1514), *alle to good* (1799), *Alle to longe* (1506), *alle a fire* (1858). In many of these *alle* (*al*) has the force of an adverb ; in others the substantive or adjective force is stronger. Cf. 288, 296, 506, 1196, 1306, 1354, 1360, 1362 f (: imperiall *adj.*), 1458, 1649, 2105, etc. — ouer al, 684. — here with alle, 567 ; her withal (+ *cons.*), 1606 ; ther with alle, 2031 ; *but* with alle, 1528 f, 2141 f (: *both* : halle *n.*) ; with-alle, 212 f (: on the walle). In the last example our MS. is alone in writing *-e*, and there is reasonable doubt whether it should be sounded. Wi., Sk. and He., however, all show it.

III. *Allë*, singular (cf. Child, § 30 ; Freudenberger, p. 35). The form *allë* in the singular is found or required in the following verses :

And how with al[le] pyne he went, 222 ;
But vp I clombe with alle payne, 1118 ;
Disesperat of alle blys, 2015.

It is of course possible to accent the first syllable in each of these verses, but it makes very rough reading.

IV. *Allë*, plural. Whether adjective or substantive, *allë* is the proper form in the plural. The regular elision or omission of *-e* before vowels takes place, and *-e* is sometimes lacking where the metre requires it. Thus, — al and some, 46 ; Of alle that they dreme to yere, 84 ; And for to stonde al in grace, 85 ; al[le] kyndes, 204 ; al[le] these, 1008 ; herd y crien alle, 1313 f (: halle *n.*) ; weren alle, 1323 ; alle wyse, 1347 ; besoughten alle, 1706 f (: falle *inf.*) ; alle thing, 1837 ; al[le] tymes, 2121 ; they were alle, 2149. — In the following examples the adverbial force seems to predominate : Or he had al ywonne hys ryghtis, 456 ; Now wil we speke al of game, 886 ; And gunne choppen al aboute, 1824.

V. But *alle* is the plural form before demonstratives, etc., when these words count as a syllable. Thus, — al youre Actes, 347 ; al the wordes, 376 ; alle the batayles, 454 ; alle the mervelouse signals, 459 ; al the pies, 703 ; al the spies, 704 ; al these three, 716 ; al the heuens sygnes, 998 ; al the men, 1167 ; alle the pepil, 1283 ; Al these armes, 1331 ; al the paleys walles, 1398 ; alle these clerkes, 1503 ; al the gestes, 1518; alle your foos, 1668 ; alle the worlde, 1721 ; alle her lestes, 1738 ; al the dores, 1952 ; alle the houses Angles, 1959 ; Alle the sheves, 2140.

> Note. — The following examples seem plural and have been registered as such :
> But for to prove in alle wyse, 1347 ;
> That alle the worlde may of hyt here, 172 ;
> In alle thing ryght as hit is, 1837.

Ten Brink (§ 255) leaves the impression that it is only before the article or other defining word that *alle* (*pl.*) is monosyllabic. Cf., however, —And al that vsed clarion, 1247. And see the following example, though *alle* here must certainly be adverbial : A fer fro hem alle be hem selue, 1215.

§ 81. The genitive plural of *al* (cf. Child, § 44 ; ten Brink, § 255) remains in *H.F.* in, — alther first, 1368 ; alderfirste, 1429 ; alther fastest, 2131. Observe in this connection *al the wonder most*, 2059.

ADVERBS AND OTHER PARTICLES.

§ 82. Anglo-Saxon adverbs in *-e* preserve their termination in *H.F.* (Child, § 69 ; ten Brink, § 246, Anm.).

Here are also included a few later analogical formations. For *blyve, inne, oute, thanne, whanne*, see § 88.

brode (A.S. brāde), 1683.
bryghte (A.S. beorhte), 503 f ; bryght[e], 1015 f (*both* : syght *n.*).
dere (A.S. dēore, W.S. dīere, dȳre), 1752.
faire (A.S. fæg(e)re, 1539 f (: contraire *n.*) ; fayre, 1630 f (: contrarie *n.*) ; fair (+ *vowel*), 1050.
faste (A.S. fæste), 497, 1675 f (: atte laste), 1865 f (: blaste *inf.*) ; fast[e], 1204, 1314, 1569, 1583, 1591, 1592, 1919, 1990, 2151 f (: kast *3 pl. pt. ind.*) ; faste hit, 2006 ; fast (+ *vowel*), 1728, 2146.
hye (A.S. hēa(h), hēage), 497 f (: ye *n.*), 973 f (: philosophye *n.*), 1599 f (: skye *n.*) ; high[e], 531, 921 ; high (+ *vowel*), 547, 914.
kouthe (A.S. cūðe), 757 f (: mouthe *n.*).

late (A.S. late), 2139.
longe (A.S. longe, lange), 1300, 1506; longe, 554, 678; longe, 1454; But hit were alle to longe to rede The names . . . 1354–5.
low[e] (O.N. lāg-r, *adj.*), 1121 f (: know *inf.*).
lowde (A.S. hlūde), 2096 f (: crowde *inf.*); lowde, 810, 1681.
nede (A.S. nȳde, nīede, nēde), 724 f (: drede *n.*), 786; cf. *nedes*, § 91.
rathe (A.S. hraðe), 2139 f (: lathe *n.*).
sharpe (A.S. scearpe), 774 f, 1202 f (*both :* harpe *n.*).
softe (A.S. sōfte), 1725 f (: on lofte).
sore (A.S. sāre), 338, 1590 f (: rore *inf.*).
stille (A.S. stille), 324.
streghte (A.S. streht, *pp.*), 1992; *but* streght to, 2111.
swifte (A.S. swifte), 1643.
swithe (A.S. swīðe), 538, 1859 f (: blithe *pred. adj. sg.*).
thikke (A.S. þicce), 1345 f (: wikke *post. adj. sg.*); thik of, 1350.
unnethe (A.S. uneaðe), 2041; cf. *unnethes*, § 91.
wide (A.S. wīde), 1488 f (: ovide *pr. n.*); 1952 f (: tyde *n.*); wide, 1139.
yerne (A.S. georne), 910 f (: discerne *inf.*).

To these may be added the Romance words *clere, pryvee* and *queynte*.

clere (O.F. cler), 1125 f (: matere *n.*), 1722 f (: here *inf.*).
pryvee (O.F. prive), 810.
queynte (O.F. cointe), 245 f (: peynte *inf.*).

Note. — For *mawgree* (O.F. malgré, maugré), *prep.*, cf. 461.

§ 83. Exceptions to § 82.

ryght (A.S. rihte), 113, 132, 358, 394, 417, 477, 561, 714, 729, 742, 780, 793, 809, 816, 874, 994, 1073, 1075 f (: wight *n.*), 1157; ryghte, 1524, 1528, 1729, 1792; ryghte, 1547, 1664. — *aryght* (A.S. on riht) has of course no *-e*: cf. 50 f, 79 f, 527 f, 2024 f (*all :* myght *n.*), 1829 f (: wyght *n.*).
lyke (A.S. gelīce), 873; lyke, 1508.

Cf. also under *longe*, § 82; and observe *streghte* in the same section.

Note 1. — For *fayn* as adv., see § 85, n. 1. For *adoun, doun,* etc., see § 88, n. 1.

Note 2. — *Yis* (A.S. gise, gese) has lost its *-e*: cf. 706, 706 f, 864 f *both :* this *pro.*), 1000, etc.

§ 84. Adverbs in *-ly, -lyche, -liche, lich* (A.S. *-līce, -lice,* O.N. *-liga*).

The evidence of the *Hous of Fame* MSS. does not bear out

ten Brink's theory (§ 270) that Chaucer was inclined to use *-lich* or *liche* before a vowel or *h*. There are all told but four verses in which these forms occur before vowels, as follows: ffullych*e* (B fullich, P fulleche, C fullych, T fullyche), 428; queynt[e]lich (B queintilich, C T queyntly), 1943; wonderlych (B wondyrly, P C T wonderly), 1173; wonderlych (B wonderlich, C T wonderly), 1922. On the other hand *-ly* occurs 12 times before vowels and 3 times before *h*; they are indicated in the following list by Gothic figures. In two verses an additional syllable is required before a consonant; in these *-liche* is manifestly the proper form: Enbrowdede wonderliche riche (*so* P; rest *wonderly*), 1327; Hir tho so wondirlich[e] streght (*so* B; rest *wonderly*), 1373. In the latter verse P C T omit *tho* and show *silf, self, selfe;* but the line as given is pretty certainly correct.

besëly, 16; boldëly, 581 f; càsuelly (*3 syl.*), 679 f; certeynly, **128, 1890, 1901**; certenly, 14 f, 994; craftëly, 1203 f; cruelly (*l.* trewëly), 1661 f; debònairly, 2013 f; derkly, 51 f; dispitously, **161**; diuersly, **1900**; dyuèrsly, 1546; ententyfly, 616 f; esëly, **1675**, 1929 f; eternally, 1403 f; falsly, 389 f; fàlsly, 392; feythfully, 853 f, 963; fully, 290, 658; fynally, 2009; gladly, 605, 1861; glàdly, 1242, 1677; goodely, 565, 1870; hardëly, 359 f; hydously, **1599**; inly, 31; kenely, **1725**; lewdely, *866; lyghtly, **546**; oònly, 57, 1743; oonly, 277, 647; oppenly, 2046 f; outterly, 1541 f; outtirly, 2014 f; perpètuelly (*4 syl.*), **1364**; prevëly, 223, 360 f; preuëly, 2045 f; purely, **39**; redëly, 130 f, 313 f, 1127 f, 1392 f, 2137 f; ryghte fully, 1662 f; savely, 291; sikerly, 1930 f; shortly, **239, 242, 257**; sothely, **364**; stedfastly, 61 f; sturmëly, 1498 f; symply, 854 f; trew[ë]ly, 615 f, 1319 f, 1542 f; tru[ë]ly, 1045 f; vnkyndëly, 295 f; vtterly, 296 f; verrayly, **1729**; wikkidly, 390 f; wisly, 1860.

Rhyme words. — I(y) (14, 51, 61, 130, 313, 581, 1045, 1127, 1319, 1392, 1403, 2137), by *adv.* (1203, 1498), why *adv.* (679), adverbs in *-ly* (the rest).

§ 85. The following adverbs which have *-e* neither in Anglo-Saxon nor in *H.F.* deserve notice:

amys (see Mätzner, p. 74), 269 f, 2079 f (*both:* is 3 *sg. pr. ind.*), 596 f (: this *pro.*), 2016 f (: blys *n.*). — anoon (A.S. on ān), 132, 339, 793, 813, 894, 69 f, 655 f, 790 f (*all:* stoon *n.*), 366 f (: agoon *pp.*), 952 f (: gon *inf.*), etc. — ful, (A.S. ful), 102, 139, 147, 214, 295, 327, 414, 581, etc. — home (A.S. hām), see § 18. — nygh (A.S. nēah, nēh), *prep.*, 1047. — streghte (A.S. streht, *pp.*), see § 82. — wis (*neut. adj.* used as *adv.*, cf. *y-wys*), Also wis god helpe me, 576 ; Nay wis quod she, 1819 ; Also wis god rede me, 1067. — y-nogh (A.S. genōg, genōh), 1032 f (: swogh *n.*). — y-wys, I-wys (A.S. gewis, *adj. neut.*), 326, 982, 809 f, 827 f, 836 f, 882 f, 1291 f, 1445 f, 1638 f, 1838 f (*all :* is (ys) *3 sg. pr. ind.*), 1470 f (Columpnis *pr. n.*), 1514 f, 1565 f (*both :* this *pro.*), 1843 f (: ysidis *pr. n.*).

The following Romance words are used adverbially without final *-e :*

apert(e) (O.F. apert), 717 f (: overte *adj. post. sing.*). Is *-e* sounded here ? — cèrteyn (O.F. certein, certain), 614, 724, 1336, 1380, 1691, 1698, 1881, 2002 ; cèrteyne, 336 ; certèyn, 929 f (: Citezeyn *n.*) ; certàyn(e), 159 f (: y- slayne *pp.*).

The following adjective formations in *-les* (A.S. -lēas) are used adverbially :

causëles, — That thou hast had loo causëles, 668 f (: rechcheles *adj.*) ; gilt[ë]les, — Shul thus be shamed gilt[ë]les (*adj. ?*), 1634 f (: pres *n.*) ; thus was her shame y-ronge And gilt[ë]les on euery tonge, 1655–6.

    Note 1. — The adjective *fayn* (A.S. fæg(e)n is used with *wolde* with the force of an adverb, — I wolde fayn han hadde a fame, 1848.

    Note 2. — For *wonder* used adverbially, *cf.* wonder sone, 114 ; wonder low, 1121 ; wonder hye, 1465 ; wonder wide, 1488 ; wonder fewe, 1691. — The adjective *famous* is similarly used in *famous good*, 1780.

    Note 3. — For *half* used adverbially (cf. A.S. healfe, *instr.* with compar.), *cf.* half so high, 914.

    Note 4. — The following adverbs, etc., of various formation, are for convenience put together here :

    ay (O.N. ei, cf. A.S. ā, āwa), 74, 467, 820, 962, etc. — eft (A.S. eft), 1072, 2038 f (: left *pp.*) ; efte, 401. — est (A.S. ēast), see *west*. — fer (A.S. feor(r)), as fer as, 483 ; ful ofte fer, 610 f (: Iupiter). — forth (A.S. forð), 795 ; forthe, 1018, 1090, 1916 ; forthe, 365 ; as ferforth as, 328 ; as fer forthe as, 1882. — nay (O.N nei), 913, 994, 1043, 1819, 2097. — noo (A.S. nā, nō), 700, 701. — northe (A.S. norð), see *west*. — south(e) (A.S. sūð), see *west*. — tho (A.S. þā), 149, 451, etc. ; thoo, 235 f (: goo *inf.*), 319 f (: doo *inf.*), 433, 496, 571, etc. — wel (A.S. wel), 129, 327, 334, etc. ; wel(e), 66 f (: euerydele) ; wele, 91 ; well(e), 1650 f (: tuelle *n.*) ; as wel as, 1442, 1739. — west (A.S. west), And blew it est and west and south(e) (: mouthe *n.*) And northe, 1680–1 ; north and south(e), 2075 f (: mouthe *n*.). — yet (A.S. giet, gyt; *also* gieta), 386, 421, 471, 580, etc.; yitt(e), 619 f, 1378 f (*both :* witte *n*.).

§ 86. Comparison of Adverbs (Child, § 70; ten Brink, § 246, and Anm.). Comparative degree.

Of the "old" adverbial comparatives, A.S. *ǣr, bet, lǣs, mā* survive in *H.F.* Other adverbial comparatives are adjective forms. (I.) *ferre, lesse, more*; (II.) A.S. comparatives in *-or* and their analogues.

bet (A.S. bet), 13, 559, 1232, 2138.
les (A.S. lǣs), *preserved in* nathëles (A.S. nā þȳ lǣs), 1181, 1734, 2073 f (: encres *n*.).
mo (A.S. mā), euer mo, 634, 1403, 1924; euermo, 2074; euer moo, 801 f (: y-goo *pp*.), 2077 f (: goo *inf*.); neuer mo, 1926.
I. ferre (A.S. fierre, fyre, *neut. comp.*), 600 f (: sterre *n*.).
less*e* (A.S. lǣsse, *neut. comp.*), neuer the less*e*, 620.
more (A.S. māre, *neut. comp.*), *20, 245, 1125, 1754; mor*e* and mor*e*, 532 f, 962 f (*both* : sore *inf*.); mor*e* and mor*e*, 818.
II. ferther (A.S. furðor), 1112, 1651.
hier (A.S. heah(h)or), *perhaps adj.*, 1117.
lenger (A.S. leng), 1912.
lyghter (A.S. lēohtor), 1289.
upper (A.S. up(p)or), 884, 961.

> Note. — For *after, aftir* (adv. and prep.), cf. 157, 256, 1040, etc.; for *hider, hyder*, cf. 1872, 1891, 1908; for *thider, thidder*, cf. 724, 837, 1906; for *whider*, cf. 602; for *yonder*, cf. 936, 1064, 1070 f (: wonder *n*.); *yonde*, 889; for *vnder* (adv. and prep.), cf. 805 f (: wounder *n*.), 964, 1919; for *er, or* (A.S. ǣr), cf. 380, 437, 456, 1055, etc.; for *or . . . or*, cf. 819; for *eyther . . . or*, cf. 4, 833; for other . . . or, cf. 1888; for *neyther . . . ne*, cf. 18, 588; for *whether . . . or*, cf. 778; for *wher* (= whether) . . . *or*, cf. 586, 981.

§ 87. No superlative adverb takes *-e* in *H.F.* (but see note below). There are no examples of *best* or *most* preceded by *the*.

best, 624, 732, 1878; most, 847; almost (A.S. ealmǣst, ælmǣst), 1143; almost*e*, 650; first, 151, 606, 811, 850, 1340, 1898; alderfirst*e*, 1429; alther first, 1368; erst, 1496, 2075; alther fastest, 2131; next, *adv.* and *prep.*, 162, 174, 1486.

> Note. — For *now at erstë* (512) we should probably read *at the firstë*; cf. P *at þe first*, C *at the fyrst*.

§ 88. The following particles, of various formation, appear sometimes or always with an *-e* (cf. Child, § 72).

In this list are thrown together, for convenience : (i.) particles in A.S. -*an*, -*on*, — *aboute, above, beforn(e), before,* *behynde, bytweene, sithe* (etc.), *withyn, withouten, -e ;* cf. *besyde ;* (ii.) particle in A.S. -*a*, — *sone ;* (iii.) *inne, oute, thanne, whan ;* (iv.) *blyve, bothe ;* (v.) *therfore, wherefore*.

> Note. — It will be observed from the following examples that in some of these words -*e* is not written; that in others it is not pronounced when written; but all of them show -*e* somewhere in Chaucer

aboute (A.S. ymbūtan, onbūtan), *adv*. and *prep*., 481, 597 f, 811 f, 1196 f, 1824 f, 1868, 2006 f, 2120 f; about[e], 1807 f, 1925; abou*te*, 799, 1397, 1526; about (+ *vowel*), 1702.

> Rhyme words. — doute *n*. (597, 811, 2006), route *n*. (1824, 2120), with oute *adv*. (1196), shout *inf*. (1807).

above (A.S. onbufan), *adv*. and *prep*., 1758 f (love *n*.), abov*e*, 805, 1360.

blyve (A.S. bi līfe), 1106 f (: descryve *inf*.), 1521 f (: hive *n*.).

bothe . . . and (O.N. báðir, *pro*., cf. A.S. bā, bā-twā), — Bothe armes and the name, 1411; Both[e] castel and the toure, 1185; Til both[e] the eyre and erthe brende, 954; Both*e* of feire speche and chidynges, 1028; And with this worde both he and y, 1046; Both of wepinge and of game, 1199; *but* Both sothe sawes and leysinges, 676.

These seem the more likely readings for the several verses cited, though some of them may have other renderings, as will be seen. In 1185 B C T show *Bothe*, P inserts *the* ; in 954 P C T omit *the*, C T writing *Bothe*.

beforn(e) (A.S. beforan), me beforn(e), 60 f (: borne *pp*.). befor*e*, 839, 1468.

behynde (A.S. behindan), *adv*. and *prep*., 238 f (: fynde *inf*.), 1214 f (: kynde *n*.), 2150; behynd*e*, 977. In 2150 F B have *behynde* by reading *begunne* for *gunne*.

besyde (A.S. be sīdan), *prep*., 73, 440, 2105.

bytwee*ne* (A.S. betwēonan), *prep*., 2028 (F B P *lack the line*).

in (A.S. inne), *prep*., 30, 70, 80, 85, 86, 121, and *passim*.

therinne (A.S. þǣr-inne), 2003 f (: gynne *inf*.).

out*e* (A.S. ūte, ūt, ūt of), 476, 480; out*e* of, 204, 1917; out of, 598, 812, 1456; ther out come, 1927.

sone (A.S. sōna), 114 f, 1532 f, 1538 f, 1773 f, 2116 f; son*e*, 288. — efte-sones, 359.

> Rhyme words. — done *ger. inf*. (114), mone *luna* (1532, 2116), bone *n*. (1538, 1773).

syth, sith, sithe, syn (A.S. siðþām, siððan). I. In causal sense : syth, 218, 1855 ; syth that, 2016 ; sithe that, 2007 ;

syn that, 835. II. Temporal : syth, 100, 1340 ; sith that 59, 1898.

thanne, than, then (A.S. þonne), temporal and illative : thanne, 368 f (: Anne) ; than (then), *before vowels and consonants*, 482, 848, 985, 1019, 1228, 1907, 2050, etc.

than = *quam* (A.S. þonne, þon), *before vowels and consonants*, 20, 977, 1289, 1290, 1371, 1638, etc.

whan, when (A.S. hwonne), *before vowels and consonants*, 112, 266, 364, 372, 393, 468, 480, 673, 774, 777, 976, 1036, 1041, 1110, 1285, etc. ; when that, 232.

therfore, therfor (A.S. þǣre + fore) : ther-fore̜, 276 ; therfore̜, 661 ; therfor*e*, 289, 990, 1355, 2001 ; therfor (+ *cons.*), 1443. — wherfore̜, 268 ; where̜ fore̜, 1835 ; wherfor*e*, 629, 641 ; wherfor (+ *cons.*), 1846.

withyn (A.S. wið-innan), *prep.* : *before vowels*, 120, 415 ; *before h*, 542.

withouten, with-outen, wythouten (A.S. wið-ūtan), 484, 830, 855, 1187, 1448, 1464, 1764, 1913.

withoute, 292, 690 ; with oute, 1195 f (: aboute *adv.*).

> Note 1. — The *-e* which is twice written in *doun, adoun* (A.S. of-dūne, adūne ; adūnweard) is unsounded : *doun*, 741 f (: sovne *n.*), 947 f (: Scorpioun *pr. n.*), 1026 f (: soun *n.*) ; *dovne̜*, 164 ; *adon*, 896 ; *adoun*, 2033 f (: congregacioun *n.*) ; *adovn(e)*, 888 f (: tovne *n.*).

§ 89. To the list in § 88 may be appended : I. *awey*[e], *betwexen*, *eke*, *ofte* ; II. *here*, *there*, *where*, and their varieties, — particles in which the form of the termination has been influenced by various analogies (cf. Child, § 72, *b*).

a-wey[e] (A.S. onweg, āweg), Yif hyt a-wey[e] be ther froo, 838 ; but *-e* is nowhere written. — awey, 317 f (: wele-away), 736, 1149, 1150 ; a-way, 418 ; away, 1145.

betwexen (A.S. betwix, betweox, betwuxt), 715 ; betwex hem, 1476.

eke (A.S. ēac, cf. tō ēacan), 624 f (: seke *3 pl. pr. ind.*) ; 1401 f (: meke *pred. adj. pl.*) ; and except that it seems so well agreed on that *eke* is never dissyllabic within the verse, one would be inclined to sound *-e* in this line : And eke ther with sothe to telle, 1804. Cf. also : And eke moo holdynge in hondes, 692. In the latter verse, however, Willert is almost certainly correct in writing *holdynges in honde.* — ek*e̜*, 179, 212, 249, 444, 570, 846, 919, 1015, etc. ; ek*e*, 193, 194, 343, 445, 752, 986, etc. ; ek(e), 1707 f (: leke *n.*).

ofte (A.S. oft), 610 ; ofte̜, 632 ; oft*e*, 385 ; oft + *vowel*), 1287.

here (A.S. hēr), 980 f (: were *n.*), 1014 f (: matere *n.*), 1912 f
(: here *inf.*) ; here, 324, 1015, 1883 ; her(e), 1444 f (: pilere
n.) ; her (+ *cons.*), 1023 ; her (+ *vowel*), 1061 ; her on
1135 ; here with alle, 567. In one case it seems likely that
we have *herë* within the verse : Be god I wolde hyt here
write, 382.

there (A.S. þǣr, þēr), 1250 f (: were *3 pl. pt. ind.*) ; there, 74,
1251 ; ther, 193, 198, 209, 212, 219, 237, 253, 308, 443, etc. ;
ther as, 113, 844 ; ther aboute, 597 ; ther-fore, 276 ; therfor*e*,
289, 990, 1355, 2001 ; ther fro, 736 f, 838 f, 895 f ; therof,
101, 1043, 1473 ; theron, 1998 ; ther out, 1927 ; ther to
(too), 371 f, 718, 998 f, 1650 ; therwith, 582, 1804 ; ther
with alle, 2031 ; ther (= *where*), 731, 2143, etc.

where (A.S. hwǣr, hwēr), 233 f (: were *3 pl. pt. ind.*); where
711, 2025 ; wher*e*, 475, 479, 1584 ; where that, 1902 ; wher
that, 129, 890, 1010 ; wherfore, 268 ; wherfor*e*, 629, 641 ;
wherfor, 1846 ; owghwher*e*, 478 ; nowher*e*, 1602.

> Note. — The rhyme-words for *here* are different from those of
> *there* and *where*.

§ 90. *Ever* (A.S. ǣfre) is in *H.F.* uniformly dissyllabic before
consonants. It does not occur before vowels, but in the two
instances before weak *h* it is monosyllabic. The invariable
spelling is *euer*.

I. Before *consonants :* 619, 634, 698, 1147, 1403, 1806, 1897,
1924, 2130.

II. Before *he, hit :* On alle that euer he myght[e] swere, 422 ;
Than euer hit was and went anoon, 2083 ; *but* Allas that
euër had[de] routhe, 332.

Never (A.S. nǣfre) before consonants is with two exceptions dissyllabic ; in the single example before a vowel it is
monosyllabic. The spelling is uniformly *neuer*.

I. Before *consonants :* 15, 59, 327, 471, 534, 566, 628, *984,
1296, 1366, 1380, 1740, 1926, 1956, 2004, 2037, 2100, 2148.
Cf. also,— That neuër herd I thing so hye, 1020. This is the
only instance before *h*. — In the two following verses *neuer*
is monosyllabic : And neuer the lesse hast set thy witte, 620 ;
And bere hit neuer so hye on hight, 740.

II. Before *vowel :* In speche and neuer a dele of trouthe, 331.
For *euer* and *neuer* in rhyme, see the following verses :

> Of olde (*l.* golde) werke than I sawgh euer
> ffor certeynly I nyste neuer, 127–8 ;
> Eke though I myght[e] dure euer
> That I haue do rekeuer I neuer, 353–4.

Note. — Two verses in which *neuer* seems monosyllabic before a consonant are easily emended by comparison of MSS.: Hyt was nyste I neuer redely, 1127; Deserue why ne neuer ye roughte, 1781. In the first of these P C T properly omit *neuer*; and in the latter the same authorities lack *ye*.

§ 91. Particles ending in *-es*, *-s* (Child, § 73). This is sometimes an A.S. *-es*, sometimes a formation by analogy.

Here also are included particles which do not in *H.F.* show a form in *-es*, but do have it elsewhere in Chaucer. (i.) *ageyn(e)* (etc.), *amyddys* (etc.), *elles*, *nedes*, *towardes*, *vnnethes*; (ii.) *hennes*, *thens*; (iii.) *ones* (*nones*), *twyes*; (iv.) *alday*, *alwey*, *eny weyes*, *other weyes*, *amonges* (*amonge*), *end[e]long(e)*, *to-geder*; (v.) *algate*, *certes*.

ageyn(e) (A.S. ongægnes, ongægn), *adv.*, 564 f (: seyne *inf.*); a-yen*e*, 544; ayen, *prep.*, 1035, 1523.
alday (A.S. ealne dæg, *adverbial acc.*), 1684, 1693, 1697; certys, 1986, 2038.
algat*e* (cf. O.N. alla götu, *adverbial acc.*), 943.
alwey (A.S. ealne weg, *adverbial acc.*), 76, 466, 744; alway, 961.
amonges (A.S. ongemang, onmang), 1633.
amyddys (cf. A.S. on middan), 845; in middes of, 714; in mid the way, 923.
certes (O.F. certes), 1684, 1693, 1697; certys, 1986, 2038.
elles (A.S. elles), 60, 234, 304, 646, 763, 908, 1039, 1741, 1940, 2046; ellis, 23, 27, 33. 425 f (: tellis *3 sg. pr. ind.*). In one case *elles* seems to be a monosyllable: Elles I wold[e] the haue tolde, 996; in the only other example before a vowel (623) it is dissyllabic.
end[e] long(e) (A.S. andlang), 1458 f (: stronge *post. adj. sg.*).
hennes (A.S. heonon, L. W. S. heonone), 1284; hennes-forth*e*, 782.
nedes (A.S. nēdes, nīedes), 1635. For *nede*, cf. § 82.
nones, see *ones*, below.
ones (A.S. ǣnes, *Chron.* 1120; ānes, *Chron.* 1131), 940, 1742; attones, 863; at ones, 2088 f (: for the nones), 2105. — for the nones, 2087 f (: at ones); wyth the nones, 2099.
thens (A.S. þanon), 1038.
to-geder (A.S. æt-gædre, tō-gædre), 2109.
towardes (A.S. tōweard), 196. Cf. doùnwarde, *746; nòrthe-warde, 1152; thiderwarde, 2144; vpwarde, 744; vpwarde, 825; vpward, 925.
twyes (A.S. twiwa, twiges, *Chron.* 1120), 573.
vnnethes (A.S. unēaðe), 900, 1140. Cf. *vnnethe*, § 82.
weyes, — Shal I noon other weyes dye, 585; Yf I koude eny weyes know, 1122.

VERBS.

§ 92. Present Indicative[1]. — The First Person Singular of the Present Indicative ends regularly in *-e* (Child, § 48; ten Brink, § 184).

I. In rhyme:
duelle, 2001 f (: telle *1 sg. pr. ind.*); fynde, 750 f (: kynde *n.*); hote, 1719 f (: note *n.*); here, 1058 f (: lere *inf.*); pace, 1355 f (: place *n.*); preve, 826 f (: meve *inf.*); rede, 77 f (: spede *inf.*), 1493 f (: brede·*n.*), 1935 f (: rede *adj. post. pl.*); seye, 673 f (: leye *inf.*); stonde, 1878 f (: honde *n.*); telle, 844 f (: duelle *inf.*), 2002 f (: duelle *1 sg. pr. ind.*); thinke, 15 f (: swinke *inf.*); trowe, 1335 f (: I-knowe *inf.*); varye, 808 f (: contrarye *n.*)

II. Before consonants.
gynne, 1455; graunte, 1665, 1763; graunte yow, 1700; stonde here (*hic*), 1885; trowe, 61, 1930.

III. This *-e* is regularly elided before a vowel:
a-legge, 314; leve, 1012; mene, 1895; pray I, 97; prey I, 78; pray alway, 466; sey I, 286, 742; stynte, 1417.

IV. Elision before *h*:
graunte hyt, 1838; preve hyt, 787.

> Note 1. — There is no certain case of apocope of *-e*. The most likely example is: But thus I sey yow trewly, 1542. The verse as it stands lacks a syllable, which may be had by writing either *sey*[*e*] or *trew*[*e*]*ly*; the latter is perhaps better. One other verse is easily emended by comparison of MSS.: I werne yow hit quod she anon, 1559. Here PC omit *hit*, T shifting the position of *hit* and *yo:v.*
>
> Note 2. — For the monosyllabic *see* (*se*), cf. *see I*, 334; *see*, 1107 f (: tree *n.*); *se*, 1910 f (: me *pro.*).

§ 93. The Second Person Singular of the Present Indicative ends in *-est* (*-ist*), *-st* (*-ęst*) (Child, § 49; ten Brink, §§ 184, 186, 259).

I. *-est* (*-ist*):
demest, 596; desirest, 1911; devisest, 637 f (: dispisest); dispisest, 638 f (: devisest); enditest, 634 f (: writest);

---

[1] It is hardly safe to claim absolute accuracy for the following sections in which a distinction between indicative and subjunctive is aimed at; the errors, however, can certainly not be numerous enough to affect the general results.

fairest, 887 ; herist, 651 ; knowest, 890 ; lyvest, 659 ; peynest, 627 ; redest, 1001 ; sittest, 657 ; suffrest, 2013 ; werest, 1840 ; writest, 633 f (: enditest).

II. *-st -est*

seyst (*vides*), 911 ; seyst (*dicis*), 1839 ; herestow, 1031, 1862.

  Note. — The ending *-es* occurs once : That thou now hider bringes, 1908 f (: tydynges).

§ 94. The Third Person Singular of the Present Indicative ends usually in *-eth (-ith), -th (-eth)* (Child, § 50 ; ten Brink, §§ 184, 186).

I. *-eth (-ith)* :

beloweth, 1803 ; causeth, 3, 815 ; considereth, 642 ; countrefeteth, 1213 ; duelleth, 70, 711 f (: tellith) ; falleth, 741 ; fareth, 271 f (: glareth); folwèth, 5 ; glareth, 272 f (: fareth) ; knoweth, 13, 290 ; longeth, 244, 1200 ; maketh, 1065, 1175 ; moveth, 735, 811, 837, 851 ; moueth, 841 ; rumbleth, 1026 ; seketh, 756 ; seweth, 840 ; sheweth, 830 ; slepeth, 74 ; stereth, 817 f (: vpbereth) ; sufficeth, 1762, 1876 ; telleth, 406 ; tellith, 712 f (: duelleth) ; vpbereth, 818 f (: stereth) ; vseth, 562 ; warneth, 46 ; wexeth, 1076 ; whirleth, 2006 ; willeth, 447.

II. *-th, -eth.*

 (*a*) Verbs ending in a vowel :

astonyeth (*slur*), 1174 ; seyth, 307, 429, 807. These are the only verbs with vowel-ending in the third person.

 (*b*) Verbs ending in a consonant :

avayleth, 363 ; breketh, 780 ; cometh, 71, 648, 721, 773, 882, 1061, 1071 ; speketh, 1244 ; thenketh (*videtur*), 871. But s[p]eketh, 931 ; thinketh (*videtur*), 684 ; to-breketh, 779 f (: men speketh).

  Note. — There is a single example of *-is :* In certeyne [as] the booke [vs] tellis, 426 f (: ellis) ; *as* and *vs* supplied from P C T.

§ 95. The following examples of the Third Person Singular in *-t* from verbs in *-t, -d* occur in *H.F.* (Child, § 51 ; ten Brink, § 186) :

grynt, 1798 ; halt, 630 ; list, 1577 ; lyst, 640, 844, 1564, 1821, 1982 ; lest(e), 1665 f (: wiste *pp.*) ; stant, 713, 719, 1117 ; stert, 681 ; writ, 973, 1385. — *But* nedeth, 575, 1072, 1299.

§ 96. The Plural of the Present Indicative ends regularly in *-en* or *-e* ; but forms in *-eth* occur (cf. Child, § 52 ; ten Brink, § 186). Before consonants *-en* is commoner than *-e* ; the reverse is true in rhyme.

I. -*en* before consonants : (*a*) *First Person*, besechen, 1554 ; (*b*) *Second Person*, knowen ye, 1257 ; ye (*tu*) knowèn (knòwen ?), 327 ; (*c*) *Third Person*, callen, 609 ; crien, 1322 ; kepen, 1226 ; maken, 1239 ; semen, 1402 ; shynen, 1376 ; tellen, 1198 ; wilnen, 1312.
II. -*en* in rhyme : *Third Person*, dreden, 38 f (: leden *3 pl. pr. ind.*) ; duellen, 1060 f (: tellen *inf.*); leden, 37 f (: dreden *3 pl. pr. ind.*).
III. -*en* before vowels : *Third Person*, hopen, 38 ; maken, 1939.
IV. *en* before *h* : (*a*) *First Person*, kepen haue, 1695 : (*b*) *Third Person*, kallen hyt, 939 ; shynen here (*hic*), 1015.
V. -*ęn, -n* : *Third Person*, clepęn a, 1326 ; redęn in, 1352 ; seyn, 1147 ; sayn(e), 23 f (: brayne *n.*). But *seyn* is the only genuine case of syncope ; both *clepęn* and *redęn* show variants in elided *-e*.
VI. -*e* before consonants : (*a*) *Second Person*, wene ye, 1714 ; (*b*) *Third Person*, calle founder, 535.
VII. -*ë* before vowel : *Third Person*, That duellë almoste at thy dors, 650. [Var. B dwell, P dwelleth, C T dwellen].
VIII. -*e* in rhyme : (*a*) *Second Person*, duelle, 521 f (: welle *n.*) ; (*b*) *Third Person*, fynde, 44 f (: kynde *n.*) ; rede, 590 f (: Ganymede) ; seke, 626 f (: eke) ; smyte 777 f (: lyte *adv.*) ; stonde, 1010 f (: honde *n.*) ; thwite, 1938 f (: white *pred. adj. pl.*).
IX. -*e* elided before vowels : (*a*) *Second Person*, gete, 1560 ; (*b*) *Third Person*, duelle, 1531 ; falle, 1192 ; seke, 744 ; trete, 54 ; vse, 1263 ; write, 1013.

> Note. — The verb *pray* shows no ending, but -*e* or -*en* is to be supplied : That natheles yet prey[e] we, 1734 ; Where fore we pray[en] yow a rowe, 1835. In the first verse P shows *preyen*, and in the second reads *on a rowe*.

§ 97. The following examples of the Plural of the Present Indicative in -*eth* occur :

causeth, 35, 40 ; men clepeth, 73 ; seyth the peple, 360 ; men speketh, 780 f (: to-breketh *3 sg. pr. ind.*). But *causeth* occurs in a confused passage and may be intended as singular.

§ 98. The Plural in -*es* does not occur in *H.F.*

§ 99. The following Indicative Preterites (first and third persons) of Anglo-Saxon verbs of the First Weak Conjugation occur in *H.F.* (cf. Child, § 53 ; ten Brink, §§ 162, 165, 168–170.

(*a*) Stems originally short, — *leyde, sette, shette*; (*b*) stems originally long, — *agylte, bilt, demed, dreynt*[*e*], *felte, ferde, hente, herde, lefte, mette* (A.S. mǣtte), *mette* (A.S. mētte), *reight*[*e*], *semed, stent*[*e*], *wente, werned;* (*c*) irregular verbs, — *broghte, duelled, soughte, streight*[*e*], *thoughte* (A.S. þōhte), *thoughte* (A.S. þūhte), *tolde*.

Of these *demed, semed, werned* are unsyncopated preterites formed on the analogy of the Second Weak Conjugation, and replacing the proper Anglo-Saxon forms *dēmde, sēmde, wyrnde*. *Duelled* corresponds to A.S. *dwelede* (*-ode*), inf. *dwelian* (Sievers, § 407, Anm. 1).

In *bilt, felte, lefte, wente*, A.S. *-de* is replaced by *-te* (cf. ten Brink, § 170 ε, ζ). *Brennen* (O.N. *brenna*, A.S *bærnan*) has only *brende;* see § 100 (cf. ten Brink, § 179, ζ).

Syncopated preterites, after the analogy of the first weak conjugation, are shown by several verbs strong in Anglo-Saxon: *brayde, fled, highte, lost* (also *les*), *slept* (also *slep*(*e*)); see § 103. So also *dyẹde* (O.N. *deyja*, pret. *dō*). For *smelde*, see § 100.

Several preterites of weak verbs belonging properly to the second conjugation show syncopated forms after the analogy of the first; see § 101.

agylte (A.S. āgyltan, āgylte), agylte yow, 329.
bilt (A.S. byldan, bylde), bilt || god, 1135.
broghte (A.S. bringan, brōhte), 2029 f (: me thoughte).
demed (A.S. dēman, dēmde), 263 f (: semed *3 sg. pt. ind.*).
dreynt[e] (A.S. drencan, drencte), 923 f (: compleynt *n.*).
duellẹd (A.S. dwelian, dwelede, dwelode, Sievers, § 407, Anm. 1), duellẹd er nowe, 1902.
felte (A.S. fēlan, fēlde), felt*e* eke, 570 ; felt that, 569.
ferde (A.S. fēran, fērde), 1932 f (: herde *1 sg. pt. ind.*) ; ferd as, 1522.
hente (A.S. hentan, hente), 543 f (: went *3 sg. pt. ind.*) ; hentè me, 2028. C T alone show the latter verse, and T omits *-e*. We should possibly read *hẹ̀ntẹ*.
herde (A.S. hīeran, hīerde), herde there, 2057 : herd*e*, 1062, *2053, 2141 ; herd ·(+ *vowel*), 1020, 1201, 1243, 1245, 1313, 1397, 1404.
lefte (A.S. lǣfan, lǣfde), left[e] not, 1600 ; left*e* hir, 295, 416 ; left hir, 403.
leyd*e* (A.S. lecgan, legde, lēde), 260.
mette (A.S. mǣtan, mǣtte), 523 f (: shette *3 sg. pt. ind.*); mette, 313, 517 ; mett*e*, 61, 119, 560 ; met or, 110.
mette (A.S. mētan, mētte), 2069 f (: lette *3 sg. pt. subj.*); mett*e* I, 1308.

reight[e] (A.S. rǣcan, rǣhte), 1374 f (. streight *3 sg. pt. ind.*).
shette (A.S. scyttan, scytte), 524 f (: mette *3 sg. pt. ind.*).
semed (A.S. ge-sēman, ge-sēmde), 264 f (: demed *3 sg. pt. ind.*); *before consonants*, 500, 1525, 2157.
sette (A.S. settan, sette), sette me, 1050; set I, 1858; set in, 2033; set hyt, 1679.
sought*e* (A.S. sēcan, sōhte), 185.
stent[e] (A.S. for-styntan, ge-stentan, *-stynte, *-stente), 221 f, 1926 f, 2031 f; stynt[e], 1683 f.
  Rhyme word. — went *pt. sg.*
streight[e] (A.S. strecc(e)an, streahte), 1373 f (: reight *3 sg. pt. ind.*).
thought*e* (A.S. þenc(e)an, þōhte), 595; thought I (y), 492, 584, 972, 985, 1631, 1852.
thoughte (A.S. þync(e)an, þūhte), 1183, 1870; thought[e], 1369: thoghte, 2030 f (: broghte *3 sg. pt. ind.*); thought*e* hit, 2031; thought I, 499.
tolde (A.S. tellan, tealde), 1380 f (: beholde *inf.*), 1434 f (: olde *adj. def. post.*); tolde Dido, 254; told*e* alle, 2046; told*e* hym, 2050; told him, 2071.
went[e] (A.S. wendan, wende), 222 f, 544 f, 1684 f, 1925 f, 2032 f, 2131 f; went*e* anoon, 1366; went (+ *vowel*), 1307, 1807, 2076, 2083. In the only two examples before a consonant -*e* is lacking; we should probably read the verses thus: Went this foule trumpes soun, 1642; That thrugh the worlde went[e̜] the soun, 1724.
  Rhyme words. — stent *3 sg. pt. ind.* (222, 1925, 2032), stynt *3 sg. pt. ind.* (1684), hente *3 sg. pt. ind.* (544), entent *n.* (2131).
werned (A.S. wyrnan, wyrnde; *probably influenced by* wearnian, wearnode), werned wel and faire, 1539.

§ 100. A few Indicative Preterites (first and third persons) of Old Norse verbs of the First weak Conjugation occur in *H.F.* To these add *smelde*, which is not found in Anglo-Saxon or Old Norse, but is probably of Germanic origin.

brende (O.N. brenna, brenda; cf. ten Brink, § 141), *intrans.*, 163 f, 537 f (*both :* descende *inf.*); *trans.*, brende the, 1844.
smelde, 1685 f (: helde *3 pl. pt. subj.*).
stert[e] (O.N. sterta, sterta), 1800 f (: hert *n.*).

§ 101. The following Indicative Preterites (first and third persons) of Anglo-Saxon verbs of the Second Weak Conjugation occur in *H.F.* (cf. Child, § 53; ten Brink, §§ 172–3):

answered, called, gladded, louede, made, reft, rovned, wondred.
To these add *caste* (Old Norse second conjugation) and *romed*, — Germanic in origin but not found in Anglo-Saxon.

answered (A.S. andswarian, andswarode), answèred noo, 1896; answèred and, 864.

called (A.S. ceallian, ceallode, from O.N. kalla, kallaða), called on, 367; called me 558.

caste (O.N. kasta, kastaða), 495 f (: at the laste); cast[e], 956 f (: atte laste).

gladded (A.S. gladian, gladode), gladded me, 962.

louede (A.S. lufian, lufode), 176; loued (+ *vowel*), 288, 370.

made (A.S. macian, macode), 646 f, 1159 f, 1890 f; made, 240, 257; made hym, 404, 413; made hir, 414; made the, 155; made welmore, 1290.

  Rhyme words. — glade *adj. pl.* (646, 1890), shade *n.* (1159).

reft (A.S. rēafian, rēafode), reft his, 457.

romed vp, 140.

rovned (A.S. rūnian, rūnode), rovned in, *2044.

wondred (A.S. wundrian, wundrode), wondred me, 1988.

§ 102. The following Indicative Preterites (first and third persons) of Anglo-Saxon verbs of the Third Weak Conjugation occur in *H.F.*, — *hadde, seyde* (cf. Child, § 53; ten Brink, § 162).

had[de] (A.S. habban, hæfde), 332, 1381; had doo, 395; had seen, 468; had herde, 2060; hadde I, 2042; had (+ *vowel*), 412, 421, 452, 456, 501, 1285, 1325, 1389.

seyde (A.S. secgan, sægde, sæde), 191 f (: preyde *3 sg. pt. ind.*), 1376 f (dyede *3 sg. pt. ind.*), 1677 f (: brayde *3 sg. pt. ind.*); seyde, 369, 595, 864, 885, 911, 1051, 1871, 1891, 1993, 2047; sayede, 573; seyde, 556, 641, 980; seyde he, 187.

§ 103. Several verbs that are strong in Anglo-Saxon show weak preterites in *H.F.* (cf. Child, § 54, *a*; ten Brink, § 167). With these include *dyede*, O.N.

brayde (A.S. bregdan, brægd, bræd), 1678 f (: seyde *3 sg. pt. ind.*); see *abreyd(e)*, § 108.

dyede (O.N. deyja, dō), 375 f (: seyde *3 sg. pt. ind.*); dyde, 380 f (: Ouyde *pr. n.*); dide, 106 f (: lyde *pr. n.*); dyed thorgh, 374.

fled (A.S. flēon, flēah), fled and, 166.

highte (A.S. hātan, heht, hēt; cf. ten Brink, § 135), *vocatus est:* highte stace, 1460; hight Triton, 1596; *vocatur:* highte Laude, 1673; hight[e] Pheton, 942; hight[e] sklaundre,

1580; hight the, 663; *vocatus* : hight*e* Achate, 226.— het(e), *vocatus est :* And eke the man that Triton het(e), 1604 f (: fete *n.*).

lost (A.S. forlēosan, forlēas), lost hys, 436, 950; lost her 1229; cf. *les*, § 108.

slept (A.S. slǣpan, slēp, North. slēpte), slept || me, 119; cf. *slep(e)*, § 108.

§ 104. One Romance verb shows a syncopated preterite after the analogy of the First Weak Conjugation (cf. Child, § 53; ten Brink, §§ 180, 182).

preyde, 192 f (: seyde *3 sg. pt. ind.*); but see *prayëd her (plur.)* 1815.

§ 105. Most verbs of Romance derivation make their preterites singular in *-ed*, without syncopation (cf. Child, § 53; ten Brink, § 179).

acheved alle, 463; aspied I, 1128; aspyed y, 1320; betrayed hir, 294; betrayed Adriane, 407; counseylled hir, 371; cried what, 2147; desired no-thinge, 425; graunted sone, 1538; graunted the, 1540; mused longe, 1287; pressed hem, 1590; sowneth (*error for* sowned), 1202; trayied Phillis, 390; touched heuene, 1375.

§ 106. The Indicative Second Person Singular of Weak Preterites ends in *-est* (cf. Child, § 53, *c;* ten Brink, § 194).

didest thou, 1846; haddest neuer, 628; madest vs, 470; madeste kynde, 584.

§ 107. The Second Person Singular of the Indicative Preterite of Strong Verbs has not been observed in *H.F.*

§ 108. In the First and Third Persons Singular of the Indicative Preterite of Strong Verbs a final *-e* is written quite commonly, but it is never pronounced.

abod(e), 1602 f (: brode *post. adj. sg.*). — abreyd(e), 110 f (: seyde *pp.*). — bad, 165, 186, 236, 430. — bar*e*, 169, 1018, 1435, 1461, 1490, 1510; bare, 172, 594. — be-cam*e*, 243. — began, 149, 435 f (: steris-man *n.*), 1340, 1652 f (: ran *3 sg. pt. ind.*). — beheld, 1520; behelde, 897, 965; beheld(e), 481 f, 539 f (*both :* felde *n.*). — blew, 1680, 2120; blewe, 1599 — bond*e*, 1590. — cam, 1874; came, 145, 564; cam(e) 480 f (: am *1 sg. pr. ind.*), 969 f (: adame *pr. n.*); come, 1690, 1771, 1927, 2061; com*e*, 1606; com(e), 1906 f (dome *n.*). — clombe, 1118. — clywe, 1702. — fel, 1772; ful, 922; fill*e*, 114. — Fleegh, 921. — fond(e), 1293 f (: honde *n.*); fonde,

141, 443, 1286; fonde, 1166, 1415; founde, 1129, 1584. — forswore, 389. — gan, 164, 190, 231, 235, 299, 311, 368, 392, 420, etc., etc.; gunne, 1658. — held, 1480; helde, 1587. — henge, 394. — knewe, 232. — lay, 112 f (: day *n.*), 558 f (: affray *n.*), 1152 f (: say *1 sg. pt. ind.*). — lat, 951; lete, 243, 418, 1598, 2117. — les, 1414 f (: goddes *n.*); cf. *lost*, § 103. — malte, 921. — quod, 319, 323, 700, 701, 707, etc., etc. — ran, 1651 f (: be-gan *3 sg. pt. ind.*). — rofe, 373. — sat, 1205. — sawgh, 127, 132, 151, 162, 163, 193, etc.; saugh, 174, 198, 212, 219, etc., etc.; saw, 296, 917, 933; say 1151 f (: lay *3 sg. pt. ind.*), 1191, 1283 f (: day *n.*); sey, 948, 989; sigh, 1161 f (: on high). — shoon, 1125, 1387, 1422; shoone, 1289; shone, 503, 530. — slep(e), 438 f (kepe *n.*); cf. *slept*, § 103. — slowe, 268, 956. — smote, 438. — songe, 1399. — spak(e), 555 f (: awake *impv. sg.*), *978 f (: bake *n.*), 1077 f (: blake *adj. post. sg.*); spake, 910; spake, 963. — stale, 418. — stank, 1654. — stood, 1116, 1464; stoode, 1869; stoode, 1162, 1163; stode, 1605; stood(e), 1507 f (: woode *adj. pred. sg.*). — swore, 2051. — toke, 1089, 1596; toke, 1637, 1865; tooke, 168, 223, 419, 464. — wrote, 380, 523. — wanne, 458. — yaf, 2021, 2114.

§ 109. The Plural of the Preterite Indicative of both Strong and Weak Verbs ends in *-en, -e,* for all persons (Child, § 55; ten Brink, § 194).

I. *-en* before consonants:
hadden grete fames, 1154; hadden myght, 2146; maden lowde, 1217; seyden certes, 1693; seyden lady, 1827: seyden mercy, 1730; seyden sooth, 1552; stoden forthe, 1451; troden fast, 2153; went[en] for (P *-en*), 441; weren sondry, 1194; weren white, 1937.

II. *-en* in rhyme:
Al these armes that ther weren
That they thus on her cote beren, 1331–2.

III. *-en* before vowels:
aqueynteden in, 250; besoughten alle, 1706; clamben vp, 2151; comen out, 1314; ffledden eke, 179; metten in, 2092; saten vnder, 1210; stoden alle, 1503; stoden other (F *stonden*), 1437; weren alle 1323; weren on, 1383; writen of, 1441; writen olde, 1515.

IV. *-en* before *h:*
beren hym, 947.

V. *-en* syncopated:
seyden they (*rest* seyde), 1708; stampen as, 2154; writen of 1504.

VI. -ë before consonants :
gonne doun, 1534 ; gonne stellifye, 1002 ; gonne wel, 944 ; gunne choppen, 1824 ; gunne crie, 1608 ; gunne crowde, 2095 ; gunne fast, 1728 ; gunne loute, 1704 ; gunne stonde, 1692 ; gunne wringe, 2110 ; hadde large, 1412 ; mette with, 227 ; nere nought, 1328 ; seyde graunte, 1536 ; seyde we, 1660.

VII. -e in rhyme :
brende, 954 f (: descende *inf.*) ; highte, 1519 f (syghte *n.*) ; kast[e], 2152 f (: fast *adv.*) ; ronge, 1398 f (: y-songe *pp.*) ; roughte, 1781 f (: ought *2 pl. pt. ind.*) ; tolde, 2143 f (: be-holde *inf.*) ; were, 173 f (: fere *n.*) ; 233 f (: where *adv.*), 1047 f (: spere *n.*), 1155 f (: [t]here *adv.*), 1249 f (: there *adv.*) ; went[e], 181 f (: went *n.*).

VIII. -e elided before vowels :
(be)gunne vp, 2150 ; fille anon, 1659 ; gonne as, 1589 ; gonne of, 2090 ; gonne vp, 953 ; gunne on, 1211 ; hadde in, 1849 ; hadde y-wrought, 1711 ; lost al, 156 ; ner of, 1423 ; sayde I, 2148 ; synge (*error for* songe) of, 1404 ; were alle, 2149 ; were almost, 1143 ; were in, 698 ; were on, 1319 ; wer a-cheked, 2093 ; wer as, 1316 ; write or, 1519.

IX. -e elided before *h* :
gonne her, 1550 ; gunne honoure, 1384 ; prayed her, 1815.

X. Apocope is not uncommon :
begunne to (P *begunnë* by omitting *to*), 1220 ; fonde they, 1810 ; made welmore (*sing. ?*), 1290 ; quod they, 1562 ; shoone ful (*sing. ?*), 1289 ; vsed clarion, 1247 ; were come, 1533 ; were lefte, 238 ; were made, 1424 ; were molte, 1149 ; were wonder, 1691 ; wer set, 1350.

§ 110. The Singular of the Present Subjunctive of both Strong and Weak Verbs ends in -*e* in all persons (Child, § 56 ; ten Brink, §§ 184, 188).

I. First Person : (*a*) *before consonants*, — er I bere the, 600 ; but I bringe the, 2003 ; (*b*) *in rhyme*, — yif I hit graunte, 1787 f (: avaunte *inf.*) ; as I leve, 875 f (: eve *n.*) ; or I ferther pace, 1112 f (: place *n.*) ; Though I hem noght be ordre telle, 1453 f (: duelle *inf.*) ; what I thynke, 1879 f (: drynke *inf.*) ; (*c*) *elision*, — al-so browke I wel myn hede, 273 ; as thryve I, 1615 ; what I drye or, 1879.

II. Second Person : (*a*) *before consonants*, — y prey the That thou a while a-bide me, 1994 ; Looke that thou warne me, 893 ; (*b*) *in rhyme*,—
. . . . so that thou take
Goode herte and not for fere quake, 603-4 ; (*c*) *elision*, —

And bere hyt neuer so hye, 740; besechen the That thou graunte vs, 1555; al-though thou thenke hyt, 806; yf that thow Throwe, on, 789.

III. Third Person: (*a*) *before consonants*, — also wis god helpe me, 576; also wis god rede me, 1067; (*b*) *in rhyme*, — also god youre soule blesse, 1612 f (: gentilesse *n.*); also god me blesse, 629 f (: humblesse *n.*); Yf hit so longe tyme dure, 303 f (: perauenture *adv.*); the whiche I prey . . . of oure sorwes lyghte, 467 f (: syghte *n.*); so god yow saue, 1760 f (haue *inf.*); god so me saue, 1135 f (: y-graue *pp.*); so god me spede, 1012 f (: nede *n.*); or he sterve, 101 f (: deserve *inf.*); (*c*) *elision*, — Though somme vers fayle in, 1098; though your loue laste a seson, 341; The whiche I prey alwey save vs, 466; Yf euery dreme stonde in his myght, 80; God turne vs, 1; the holy Roode turne vs, 58; wel worth of this thynge, 53; pray I . . . that euery harme . . . befalle hym, 101; bid him how that he Brynge his other clarioun, 1579; devyne he, 14; dreme he barefote dreme he shod, 98; who-so . . . mysdeme hyt, 97; And he that mouer ys of alle . . . so yive hem . . . and shelde hem . . . and send hem, 83, 88, 90; That euery man wene hem at ese, 1767.

§ 111. Exceptions to § 110.

I. First Person: Ioues . . . wol that I bere the, 662.

II. Second Person: y prey the That thou . . . lete me seen, 1995; So that thou yeve thyn aduertence, 709.

III. Third Person: Ywel thrifte come to your Iowes, 1786; helpe me god, 700; God saue the lady, 1310; god of heuen sende the grace, 1087.

§ 112. The Plural of the Present Subjunctive of both Strong and Weak verbs ends in -*e*, *en* (Child, § 56; ten Brink, §§ 184, 188).

I. Second Person:

..... how that ye determynen
And for the more parte diffynen, 343–4.

II. Third Person: (*a*) While that they fynde loue of stele, 683; (*b*) Ne hyt mysdemë in her thoght, 92; (*c*) So yive hem ioy that hyt here, 83 f (: to yere); (*d*) Or they espie hyt, 706; That take hyt wele and skorne hyt noghte, 91.

III. Apocope of -*e*: Come we morwë or on eve, 2106; yive hem ioy . . . . Of alle that they dreme to yere, 84. But in the latter verse *alle* may mean *omnia*; in that event it would be possible to read: Of alle that they dremè to yere.

I. First Conjugation : (*a*) short stems :
telle (A.S. tele), telle me, 853 ; tellè me, 2049 ; tell*e* vs, 1563.
  But telle me, 870, 1056.
II. First Conjugation : (*b*) long stems :
hid*e* (A.S. hȳd), hid*e* our, 1696.
kythe (A.S. cȳð), Now kythe thyn engyne and [thy] myght, 528. Such is pretty certainly the proper reading for this verse, *thy* being supplied after P T. It seems a little strange that Wi., Sk. and He. disregard this variant, showing *kythë*.
ringe (A.S. hring), ringe this, 1720.
spede (A.S. spēd), spede the, 1595.
  Note. — For *drede*, imperative of *dreden* (weak in Chaucer), cf. *drede the*, 1043.
III. Second Conjugation :
herkene, herke (A.S. heorcna, hercna), herkene wel, 725 ; herke be, 613 ; herke wel, 1030 ; herke what, 764.
hye (A.S. higa), 1592 f (: crie *inf.*).
looke (A.S. lōca), looke that, 893 ; loke thou, 927.
make (A.S. maca), mak*e* hyt, 1097.
IV. Third Conjugation :
haue (A.S. hafa), haue pitee, 316.
sey (A.S. saga), sey these, 1793.
V. Two Old Norse verbs :
cast (O.N. kasta), cast vp, 935.
trust[e] (O.N. treyst), trust[e] wel, 672.
§ 116. The Imperative Second Person Singular of Verbs of Romance origin ends in *H.F.* in -*e* (cf. ten Brink, § 189).
graunt he, 102 ; graunt*e* vs, 1536, 1609, 1773 ; gye, 1093 f (: maistrye *n.*) ; sav*e* and, 494 ; turn*e* vpward, 925.
§ 117. The Imperative Second Person Singular of Strong Verbs has in *H.F.*, as in Anglo-Saxon[1], no -*e* (Child, § 58 *b* ; ten Brink, § 189).
  In the following list -*e* is oftener written than otherwise, but it is regularly unsounded.
awak(e), 556 f (: spake *3 sg. pt. ind.*) ; awake to, 560. — beholde this, 926. — blow her, 1626 ; blowe this, 1790 ; blowe thy, 1718 ; blowe as, 1766 ; blowe yt, 1673. — come forth, 1912. — goo blowe, 1790 ; goo noght, 317. — farewel, 1085. — lat a, 1037 ; lat be, 992 ; lat goo, 741 ; lat me, 2097 ; lat oure, 1610 ; lat vs, 1745 ; let me, 2097 ; let our, 1556 ; let vs, 1755 ; leet men, 1761 ; late now, 1670. — rys*e*

---
[1] Short stems in -*jo* excepted ; cf. Sievers, § 372.

§ 113. The Preterite Subjunctive Singular of Strong Verbs end in -*e*; but in *H.F.* the examples are few and inconclusive. The Preterite Subjunctive Singular of Weak Verbs shows in the first and third persons the endings -*de*, -*te*, -*ed* (cf. Child § 56; ten Brink, § 195). The Second Person Singular of the Subjunctive of Weak Preterites has not been observed.

I. Strong Verbs: (*a*) *First Person*, — though I knew he places, 1014; as I were a larke, 546; (*b*) *Third Person*, — prayed her . . . that she . . . yeve hem, 1817; were, 251, 702, 1132, 1333, 1354, 1518, 1819, 1999. — *Exceptions*: (*a*) *Second Person*, — as thou were woode, 202; (*b*) *Third Person*, — or he toke kepe, 437; That hem were leuest, 87; Were the tydinge sothe or fals, 2072; nor hyt were to louge, 381; as he were woode, 1508.

II. Weak Verbs: (*a*) *First Person*, — yf I wolde her names telle, 1505; (*b*) *Third Person*, — or he lette, 2070 f (: mette *3 sg. pt. ind.*); Tyl he haue caught that what him lest[e], 282 f (: the fayrest), — but T alone shows the verse; so she saved hym hys life, 423. — Haue: (*a*) *First Person*, — As ferforth as I had[de] wytte, 328; (*b*) *Third Person*, — Though that Fame had al the pies, 703; had he lawghed had he loured, 409; had hyt stonde, 1928; Yf Adriane ne had y-be, 411. — *Exceptions*: prayed her . . . that she nolde doon, 1816; As she had been, 229.

§ 114. The Plural of the Preterite Subjunctive of both Strong and Weak Verbs ends, like that of the Present, in -*e*, *en* (cf. Child, § 56; ten Brink, § 195).

As men a potful of bawme helde, 1686 f (: smelde *3 sg. pt. ind.*); though they were of, 1850 (*ind. ?*); seyden they yeven noght a leke, 1708. — *Exceptions*: as men had writen hem, 1156; As we had wonne hyt, 1751; men wend that, 1796; as they were wode, 1809.

§ 115. The Imperative Second Person Singular of Weak Verbs follows the Anglo-Saxon inflections in the First and Second Conjugations, — that is, verbs of the Second Conjugation have -*e* (A.S. -*a*), and verbs of the First Conjugation either end in -*e* (A.S. -*e*) or have no ending, according as the stem-syllable was originally short or long. But in the two examples of verbs of the Third Conjugation -*e* is unsounded or dropped. (Cf. Child, § 58; ten Brink, § 189).

vp, 1592. — see quod, 888 ; se her, 1023 ; se yonder, 936. — slee me, 317. — stondẹ no, 1912. — vnderstond now, 1073. — yivẹ vs, 1558. — *And also* tak(e), 1673 f (: blake *adj. sg. pred.*) ; takẹ forth, 1624 ; takẹ thy, 1594 ; takẹ thyn, 1052 ; takẹ hede, 787 ; takẹ out, 1765 ; takẹ yt, 822. — *Short* -jostem, — bid (A.S. bide), bid hym, 808 ; bid him, 1573, 1578.

But in one verb *-e* is certainly pronounced : And seyde *walke* forth a pace, 1051.

> Note 1. — In these two examples *let* is doubtless to be regarded as imperative plural : let see (= *videamus*), 580 ; let vs speke (= *dicamus*), 293.
>
> Note 2. — Observe the ellipsis of the verb in *vp the hede*, 1021.

§ 118. The Imperative Second Person Plural of Verbs, strong or weak, native or naturalized, ends in *H.F.* in *-eth, -ẹth* ; but forms in *-e* and forms with no inflectional ending also occur (cf. Child, § 59 ; ten Brink, § 189).

I. Forms in *-eth, -ẹth :* entreth in, 1109 ; haueth of, 325 ; helpẹth || that, 521 ; herkẹneth as, 109 ; herkẹneth euery, 509 ; listẹneth of (P *listeth*, T *lysteth ;* and so perhaps *3 pl. pr. ind.*), 511 ; trusteth wele, 66.

II. Form in *-e :* herke how, 1549.

III. Forms without ending : goo your, 1561, 1622 ; let your, 1701 ; syker be ye, 1978.

§ 119. The infinitive ends in *H.F.* in *-en, -ẹn, e, -ẹ* (cf. Child, § 60 ; ten Brink, § 190). In *to done, to goone, to seyne*, the *-ne* of the A.S. gerund or dative-infinitive is preserved.

> The following summary is of some interest as showing the relative frequency of *-en, -ẹn, -e, -ẹ*, in the several positions : (*a*) *before consonants,* — en (26), -e (43), -ẹ (4) ; (*b*) *in rhyme,* — -en (3), -e (196) ; (*c*) *before vowels,* — -en (20), -ẹn (5), -ë (9), -*e* (54) ; (*d*) *before h,* — -en (4), -ë (2), -*e* (20). From this it will be seen that *-e* is much the commoner ending of the infinitive everywhere.

I. *-en* before consonants : abyden the, 1086 ; aprochen blyve, 1521 ; beten the, 1044 ; casten no, 1170 ; casten with, 1048 ; crien lowde, 2096 ; ensuren the, 2098 ; envien loo, 1231 ; heren that, 1024 ; heren wel, 879 ; leten wel, 1950 ; loken thoo, 896 ; menen this, 1104 ; pipen bet, 1232 ; powren wonder, 1121 ; proven the, 808 ; romen til, 1293 ; tellen can, 1324 ; tellen certeyn, 1731 ; tellen the, 726, 1884 ; tellen yow, 1343 ; tellen yowe, 1418 ; trowen this, 699 ; trumpen Messenius, 1243 ; wexèn saugh, 1391.

II. *-en* in rhyme : duellen, 1300 f (: tellen *inf.*) ; tellen,

1059 f (: duellen *3 pl. pr. ind.*) ; tellen, 1299 f (: duellen *inf.*).

III. *-en* before vowels : bilden on, 1133 ; beholden eke, 1755 ; blasen out, 1802 ; carien a, 1280 ; choppen al, 1824 ; crien alle, 1313 ; excusen Eneas, 427 ; hangen ought, 1782 ; loken vnder, 964 ; lyen euerychon, 1717 ; passen eueryche, 975 ; puffen and, 1866 ; serven in, 1548 ; shenden al, 1016 ; semen euery, 1291 ; stonden in, 1238 ; tellen also, 1388 ; tellen anon, 2062 ; wexen in, 979 ; wondren in, 583.

IV. *-en* before *h* : helpen hem, 1439 ; stonden hym, 1214 ; trumpen [hit], 1864 ; wexen hit, 1652.

V. *-ęn*, syncope : mountęn || and, 953 ; makęn || in, 1268 ; pleyęn || and, 2133 ; pleyęn vpon, 1201 ; temęn vs, 1744.

> Note. — The MSS. are at one only in 2133 ; in the other verses (except 1744) there are variants in *-e*, which of course elides before the vowels that follow; and in 1201, 1744 there is authority for reading *on* instead of *vpon*, whence we should have *pleyen, temen*.

VI. *-e* before consonants : beholde more, 532 ; bere tho, 1597 ; clymbe greued, 1119 ; come hyder, 1891 ; come to, 735 ; compleyne thanne, 368 ; confirme my, 761 ; deserue why, 1781 ; fele wel, 826 ; graunte yowe, 1822 ; helpe to, 1102 ; here many, 1915 ; here where, 711 ; holde yow, 324 ; kenne myght, 498 ; kepe that, 215 ; lerne loue, 1235 ; lerne saugh, 1250 ; loke nowe, 580 ; make folke, 42 ; make lenger, 1282 ; make lythe, 118 ; make songes, 622 ; make yow, 1300, 1454 ; passe with, 2011 ; peyne me, 246 ; rede many, 448 ; shewe yow, 1102 ; speke more, 245 ; teche the, 2024 ; telle first, 850 ; telle [the], 1792 ; telle the, 249, 894 ; telle where, 479 ; telle yow, 150, 547 ; trumpe there, 1250 ; vnderstonde kan, 510 ; vnderstonde my, 710 ; warne the, 1068 ; wynne sone, 2115.

> Note. — The following infinitives require an additional syllable, for all of which there are variants in *-e, -en* : comfort tho (235), pley Iugelours (1259), shew craft (1100), tel can (334, 450), tel fonde (1427), tel she (242).

VII. *-e* in rhyme: abrayde, 559 f (: seyde *3 sg. pt. ind.*); appere, 190 f (: here *inf.*) ; agryse, 210 f (: aryse *inf.*) ; aryse, 209 f (: agryse *inf.*) ; bede, 32 f (: drede *n.*) ; bete, 570 f (: hete *n.*) ; come, 45 f (: some *pro.*) ; drenche, 205 f (: wenche *n.*) ; 16, 64, 78, 87, 90, 102, 164, 180, 189, 195, 205, 220, 231, 237, 239, 246, 251, 252, 279, 297, 311, 381, 382, 385, 392, 413, 422, 434, 446, 447, 474, 491, 499, 508, 511, 512, 520, etc., etc., etc. — Final *-e* is to be supplied in the following examples ; in every case, indeed, there are variants which show it : blow, 1639 f (: ouerthrowe *inf.*) ; cary, 574 f (: Mary) ; cast, 1147 f (: last *inf.*) ; groon, 338 f (: euerychoon *pro.*) ; know, 1122 f (: low *adv.*) ; last, 1147 f (: cast *inf.*) ; let, 1954 f (: vnshet *pp. plur.*) ; shout, 1808 f (: about *adv.*).

VIII. -*e* elided before vowels : beholde vpon, 1111 ; bere vp, 1439, 1472 ; blowe in, 1818 ; cause another, *794 ; come in, 2005 ; countrepese ese, 1750 ; crepe at, 2086 ; dreme of, 22 ; endyte and, 520 ; 67, 79, 202 (*bis*), 216, 247, 277, 289, 293, 431, 491, 599, 705, 790, 867, 946, 958, 993, 1017, 1037, 1053, 1055, 1108, etc., etc.

IX. -*e* elided before *h* : bere hyt, 1474 ; blowe her, 1722 ; bring his, 1573 ; cache his, 404 ; countrefet hym, 1212 ; ese her, 1799 ; here hyt, 1038 ; kembe hyr, 136 ; kepe hir, 192 ; knowe hit, 377, ley hyt, 291 ; loue hym, 270 ; preyse hys, 627 ; shake hem, 868 ; shewe hym, 867 ; slepe hir, 76 ; synge hyt, 2138 ; telle hyt, 2073 ; wete his, 1785 ; wringe hir, 299.

X. Apocope of -*e* : come to, 786 ; further the, 2023 ; put the, 598 ; trumpe Ioab, 1245.

XI. Hiatus : blowë out, 204 ; durë euer, 353 ; lernë in, 1088 ; spekë al, 886 ; stondë al, 85 ; stondë in, 1692 ; stondë out, 1456 ; tellë al, 1829 ; thynkë hyt, 387 ; vnderstondë hyt, 50 ; yevë eche, 2112.— But variants in -*en* are found in 204, 387, 886, 1692.

XII. *fle, se* : fle for, 2109 ; flee ful, 610 ; flee so, 973 ; flee the, 186 ; flee, 165 f (: he), 934 f (: meynee *n.*) ; fleen, 2118 f (: seen *inf.*). — se hyt, 386 ; se men, 1106 ; se the, 533 ; se, 476 f, 525 f, 737 f, 928 f ; see darst, 580 ; see hyt, 211 ; see owghwhere, 478 ; see wel, 793 ; see with, 1492 ; see, 441 f, 483 f, 804 f, 1120 f, 1387 f, 1501 f, 1526 f, 1623 f, 1892 f ; seen, 1948 f, 1995 f (*both* : been *3 pl. pr. ind.*), 2117 f (: fleen *inf.*).

XIII. Gerundial infinitives, — *to done, to goone, to seyne* :
to done, 113 f (: sone *adv.*), 361 f (: moone *n.*) ; to doo good, 1714 ; to do al, 611 ; to do the, 664 ; to do thys, 603 ; *inf.*, do no, 1794 ; do so, 2099 ; do than, 2020 ; do, 261 f ; doo eftesones, 359 ; doo no, 1795 ; doo, 243 f, 320 f ; doon hem, 1816 ; doon vs, 1748.
to goone, 1165 f (: woone *n.*) ; to goon, 1916 f (: many oon), 2084 f (: anoon *adv.*) ; to goo by, 749 ; to goo, 1598 f (: thoo *adv.*) ; *inf.*, go as, 1106 ; go first, 2097 ; go, 2100 f ; goo in, 639 ; goo into, 430 ; goo out, 476 ; goo thyn, 741 ; goo, 197 f, 236 f, 420 f, 1950 f, 2078 f, 2094 f ; goon and, 934 ;

goon there, 2117; goon, 951 f, 1569 f, 1670 f (*all:* anoon *adv.*), 1583 f (: stoṇ *n.*); gon, 1090 f (: anon *adv.*), 1934 f (: ston *n.*), 1992 f (: stoon *n.*); for-goon, 1856 f (: oon *num.*).

sothe for to seyne, 690 f (: demeyne *inf.*); soth for to seyn(e), ageyne *adv.*); soth for to seye, 1368 f (: y-seye *pp.*); sothe to sey[e], 1917 f (: valey *n.*); *inf.*, sey[e], 713 f (wey *n.*).

§ 120. The Present Participle ends in *H.F.* in *-ynge* (*-inge*), *-yng* (*-ing*) (cf. Child, § 64; ten Brink, § 191). The only example in rhyme is with noun in *-ynge*. The examples before a consonant are few, but in these *-e* is unsounded.

I. In rhyme: goynge, 799 f (: sterynge *n.*). — II. Before consonants: dwellynge, 608; syttynge, *1415; wepynge, 214. — III. Before vowels: blowynge, 230; causynge, 796; crying (*error for* carynge), 545; cryìnge, 170; encresing, 2077; entryng, *1527; feynynge, 1478; fletynge, 133; fleynge, 543; goynge, 228; lepynge, 1823; multiplyinge, 801; pleyinge, 1252; rennynge, 2145; seyllynge, 903; sittỳng, 1394. — IV. Before *h:* wenynge hyt, 262.

§ 121. The Perfect Participle of Weak Verbs ends in *H.F.* in -ed, -ed, -d, -t (cf. Child, § 62; ten Brink, §§ 163, 166-9, 176, 180-3).

There is in *H.F.* no case of a participle rhyming with the preterite of a weak verb; the only apparent example — herde, 1932 f (: ferde *3 sg. pt. ind.*) — is shown by comparison of MSS. to be a preterite. There are three instances of final sounded *-e*, all plural: dreyntë were, 233; vnbrendë were, 173; vnshet[te], 1953 f (: let *inf.*), — *the rest* vnshette, lette.

I. Anglo-Saxon verbs of the First Conjugation (cf. § 99). agaste, 557; a-sweued, 549 f (: heued *n.*); betyd, 384; betyde, 680; betydde, 578, *2048; broght, 155; herd, 1059, 1929, 2135; herde, 1909; herde, 2060; heryed (*dissyl.*), 1405; left, 2038 f (: eft *adv.*); lefte, 238; y-ment, 1742 f (: sent *pp.*); red, 347, 722; rent, 776: sent, 612 f (: comaundement *n.*), 1741 f (: y-ment *pp.*); y-sent, 984 f (: entendement *n.*); set, 620, 845, 1350; silde (*error for* fylde), 1957; soght, 626; tolde, 2136; tolde, 823; told(e), 529 f (: golde *n.*), 996 f, 2063 f (*both:* olde *adj. sg. pred.*); tyd, 255; y-went, 976 f (: element *n.*); wroght, 1317, 1498; I-wrought, 1298; y-wrought, 1173 f, 1923 f (*both:* thought *n.*), 1711 f (: nought *pro.*). — From the Old Norse First Conjugation: brent, 2080; y-brent, 940.

II. Anglo-Saxon verbs of the Second Conjugation (cf. § 101).
axed, 1766; called, 1357; y-called, 1363 f (: y-stalled *pp.*);
cleped, 1400, 1575, 1625, 1921; clothed, 1078; Crammed,
2129; y-hated, 200; made, 592, 1362, 1424, 1922: made,
1224, 1936, 2016; y-made, 120; y-made, 691; maked, 924;
y-marked, 1103; of thowed, 1143; opened, 1952; rovned,
722, 1030 f (: compovned *pp.*); y-rovned, 2107 f (: compovned *pp.*); shamed, 1634; y-shamed, 356; shewed,
1095 f (: lewed *pred. adj. sg.*); warned, 51; wont, 2078;
wonte, 113, 566, 1548; wonte, 1581; wonde, 1576.
III. Verbs of Germanic origin which are not found in Anglo-Saxon (cf. § 101).
dasewyd (cf. O.N. dasask), 658; loured, 409 f (: devoured
pp.); piped, (cf. A.S. pīpe, *n.*), 785; twyst, 775.
IV. Anglo-Saxon verbs of the Third Conjugation (cf. § 102).
had, 667; hadde, 1848; sayde, 2052; seyde, 565, 883, 2008;
seyde, 355, 372; seyd(e), 109 f (: abreyde *1 sg. pt. ind.*).
V. Weak participles from strong verbs (cf. § 103).
adrad, 928; highte, 226; lawghed, 409; lost, 234; y-lost,
1257; y-loste, 183.
VI. Syncopated participles from verbs of Romance origin
(cf. § 104).
enclyned, 828; keuered, 275, 352; recouerd, 1258; quyt, 1614
f (: hyt *pro.*). But better, perhaps, *keuered, recouer[e]d.*
VII. Unsyncopated participles from verbs of Romance origin
(cf. § 105).
a-cheked (O.F. eschec), 2093; acheued, 1738; arryved, 1047;
assayled, 158; assured, 581; astonyed (*trisyl.*), 549; compovned, 1029 f (: rovned *pp.*), 2108 f (: y-rovned *pp.*);
conserued, 732; conserved, 1160; corovned, 1316; departed,
2068; deserued, 1613, 1662, 1545 f, 1621 f (*both :* serued,
pp); devoured, 410 f (: loured *pp.*); enbrowded, 1327;
enclyned, 749, 825; entremedled, 2124; escaped, 167;
formed, 1366, 2039; yformed, 490; founded, 1981; graunted,
220; Iuged, 357; meved, 813 f (: preved *pp.*); perched
(O.F. perche), 1991; peynted, 211, 1458; plated (O.F.
plate), 1345; preised, 1577; preved, 839, 854, 814 f
(: meved *pp.*); preued, 874; receyved, 339 f (: disceyved
pp.); served, 337, 616; serued, 1622 f (: deserued *pp.*);
y-stalled, 1364 f (: y-called *pp.*); vsed, 1242.

§ 122. The Perfect Participle of Strong Verbs ends in *H.F.* in
-*en*, -*en*, -*n*, -*e* (cf. Child, § 61; ten Brink, §§ 130, 132, 139,
140, 142, 143, 145, 148-151, 153, 155-158, 160).

I. *-en, -n*, in rhyme : born(e), 59 f (: beforne *prep.*), 345 f (: lorne *pp.*); ybroken, 765 f (: yspoken *pp.*); lorn(e), 346 f (: borne *pp.*); seyn(e), 501 f (: certeyne *adj. post. sg.*); y-slayn(e), 159 f (: certayne *adv.*); yspoken, 766 f (: ybroken *pp.*).

II. *-en* unsyncopated : blowen, 774, 1859 ; y-comen, 1074 ; corven, 1295 ; flowen, 905 ; graven, 212 ; growen, 1353 ; knowen, 757, 1676 ; leten, 1934 ; seën, 468 ; shapen, 1985 ; y-sowen, 1488 ; spoken, 881 ; y-spoken, 810 ; throwen, 1325 ; woxen, 2082 ; writen, 142, 1153.

III. *-en* syncopated : seen, 977, 2037 ; spoken [in], 717 ; sworn(e), 322 ; woxen on, 1494 ; writen hem, 1156.

IV. *-e* in rhyme : begonne, 677 f (: wonne *pp.*) ; behewe, 1306 f (: shewe *inf.*) ; beholde, 1285 f (: yholde *pp.*); ybete, 1041 f (: swete *inf.*) ; y-blowe, 1139 f (: knowe *inf.*), 1664 f (: knowe *pp.*) ; y-broke, 770 f (: smoke *n.*) ; y-colde (*error for* yholde), 1286 f (: beholde *pp.*) ; y-graue, 1136 f (: saue *3 sg. pr. subj.*) ; knowe, 1663 f (y-blowe *pp.*) ; y-knowe, 1770 f (: blowe *inf.*) ; y-ronge, 1655 f (: tonge *n.*) ; ronne, 1644 f (: gonne *n.*) ; y-seye, 1367 f (: seye *inf.*) ; songe, 347 f, 722 f (*both* : tonge *n.*) ; y-songe, 1397 f (: ronge *3 pl. pt. ind.*) ; y-sprong[e], 2081 f (: tong *n.*) ; wonne, 678 f (: begonne *pp.*).

V. *-e* before consonants : come there, 673 ; graue was, 256 ; take for, 309.

VI. *-e* apocopated : come to, 1603 ; founde || that, 2054 ; y-swore to, 421.

VII. *-e* elided before vowels : y-bor*e*, 590 ; com*e*, 1533 ; grav*e*, 157, 451 ; molt*e*, 1145, 1149 ; spok*e*, 723 ; spreng*e*, 2079 ; wonn*e*, 159.

VIII. *-e* elided before *h :* grav*e* how, 253, 433 ; tak*e* hir, 424 ; wonn*e* hyt, 1751 ; ywonn*e* hys, 456 ; wox hir, 1146.

IX. Hiatus : gravë in, 473 ; stondë vpon, 1928 ; vnknowë ys, 270. But in two of the three examples there are variants in *-en*.

§ 123. Preteritive Presents.

A.S. witan. — *1 sg. pr. ind.*, wot I, 52 ; wote wel, 980 ; wote my, 1878 ; wote I, 474 ; wotë euer (*manifest error for* wiste), 1897. — *2 sg. pr. ind.*, wost, 729, 762, 781, 790, 863, 982 f (: gost *n.*), etc. ; wostow, 1000, 1784, 1791. — *3 sg. pr. ind.*, wote why, 680 ; forwote that, 45. — *2 pl. pr. ind.*, wete ye, 1618. — *1 sg. pt. ind.*, wiste what, 1159 ; wyst*e* I, 129 ; wiste, 1544 f (: nyste *1 sg. pt. ind.*). — *3 sg. pt. ind.*, wyste sothely, 364 ; wiste that, 393. — *Pp.*, wist(e), 351 f (: miste *n.*), 1666 f (: leste *3 sg. pt. ind.*).

A.S. nytan. — *1 sg. pr. ind.*, not 12, 982, 1887, 2148. — *2 sg. pr. ind.*, nostow, 1010 ; nost not thou, 2047. — *1 sg. pt. ind.*, nyste neuer, 128 ; nyste how, 548 ; nyst[e] how, 1049, 1901 ; nyste I, 1127 ; nyste, 1543 f (: wiste *1 sg. pt. ind.*).

A.S. āgan. — *3 sg. pt. ind.*, ought[e] the, 860 ; ought him, 1134. — *3 pl. pt. ind.*, ought[e], 1782 f (: rought *2 pl. pt. ind.*). The several examples are all present in sense.

A.S. cunnan[1]. — *Inf.*, kunne gynne, 2004. — *1 sg. pr. ind. and subj.*, kan, 15, 64, **143** f, **277** f, 334 f (*all* : man *n.*), 248, 707, etc. ; can, 547, 865 f, 1324 f (: *both* : man *n.*),.etc. — *2 sg. pr. ind.*, canst, 624. — *3 sg. pr. ind.*, kan, 510 f (: man *n.*), 959, etc. — *1 pl. pr. ind.*, konne noon, 335. — *2 pl. pr. ind.*, konne groon, 338. — *3 pl. pr. ind.*, konne wel, 1265 ; kan synge, 2138 ; kan, 450 f (: Claudian). — *1 sg. pt. ind. and subj.*, koude know, 1452 ; Yf I koude eny weyes know, **1122**; koude I, 1140. — *3 sg. pt. ind.*, kouthe gesse, 1814 ; who so koude I-knowe, **1336**; kouude no 945 ; coude hem, 1797. — *3 pl. pt. ind.*, coude casten, 1170.

A.S. durran. — *1 sg. pr. ind.*, dar wel, 598 ; dar I, 674 ; dare I, 2054. — *2 sg. pr. ind.*, darst thou, 580.

A.S. sculan. — *1 sg. pr. ind.*, shal, 150, 355, 357, 585, 713, etc. — *2 sg. pr. ind.*, shalt, 577, 602, 672, 711, 793, etc. ; shaltow, 2026. — *3 sg. pr. ind.*, shal, 6, 107, 279, 308, 309, etc. ; shall(e), 82 f (alle *omnia*). — *2 pl. pr. ind.*, shul, 512, 1667, 1717 ; shal, 1615, 1619. — *3 pl. pr. ind.*, shal, 525, 1616 ; shul, 1634. — *1 sg. pt. ind. and subj.*, shuld[e] both, 1892 ; shulde I, 245, 1341 ; shulde y, 1513 ; shuld I, 1282 ; shulde the, **559**. — *3 sg. pt. ind. and subj.*, shulde drenche, 205 ; shulde shenden, **1016**; shuld[e] not, 756 ; shuld[e] fast, **1569**; shulden be, 869.

A.S. *mugan. — *2 sg. pr. ind.*, maist, 737, 2025 ; mayst, 826 ; maiste goo, 639 (*subj. ?*) ; maistow, 699, 1024 ; mayste thou, 747. — *3 sg. pr. ind. and subj.*, may, 32, 90, 274, 291, **324, 479,** 487, 587, 732, 1721, etc. — *1 pl. pr. ind.*, may not, 1759. — *2 pl. pr. ind.*, mowe here, 1828. — *2 sg. pr. subj.*, al[though] thou mowe hyt not y-see, 804. — *1 pl. pr. subj.*, pray we That we mowe han, 1735. — *1 sg. pt. ind. and subj.*, myghte see, 1501 ; though I myght[e] dure, **353** ; myght[e] see, 483 ; myght[e] not, 909 ; myght I, 2117 ; myght see, 1492. — *3 sg. pt. ind. and subj.*, myght[e] do, 261 ; myght[e]

---

[1] Of the remaining verbs of this section distinctions of mood are particularly hard to draw for *cunnan*, *sculan*, **mugan*. Often no distinction is attempted; in such cases Gothic figures indicate the more likely subjunctives.

swere, 422; myght[e] make, 1334; myght ther, 1337; myght agryse, 210; myght I, 498; myght oute, 2085; myght hyt, 763; myght hit, 1164; myght hyt, 1929.

A.S. mōtan. — *3 sg. pr. ind.*, mot to, 720, mote oute, 2139. — *1 sg. pr. subj.*, mote y, 1329. — *3 sg. pr. subj.*, mote hit, 102; mot be, 1663. — *3 sg. pt. ind. (as present)*, most[e] rede, 448; most[e] thider, 724; *(as pret.)*, most[e] nedes, 1635; most vnto, 187; most out, 2094. — *1 sg. pt. subj. (as present)*, most I, 1506. — *3 sg. pt. subj. (as pret.)*, moste haue, 410.

§ 124. Anomalous Verbs: *be, wol, nyl, do, go, haue*.

be. — *Infinitive*, be, 274, 309, 355, 356, 671, 771, 977, 1570, 1663, 1701, 1780, 2101, 2136; be, 308 f, 357 f, 418 f, 732 f, 1017 f, 1258 f, 1563 f, 1577 f, 1635 f, 2157 f; ben, 1172, 1270, 1330, 2037. — *1 sg. pr. ind.*, am, 582, 588, 608, 980, etc.; am, 479 f (: came *1 sg. pt. ind.*), 601 f (: cam *1 sg. pt. ind.*), etc. — *2 sg. pr. ind.*, art, 199, 492, 895, etc.; arte noyouse, 574; artow, 1872. — *3 sg. pr. ind.*, is, 2, 7, 29, 51, 52, etc.; ys, 45, 81, 292, 300, etc.; cause is, 20 f (: causis *n.*); wone is, 76 f (: sones *n.*), etc.; ys, 270 f, 881 f, etc.; nys, 1957, 2038; nys, 349 f, 913 f, 1063 f. — *1 pl. pr. ind.*, be, 337, 340; be, 1553 f (: the *pro.*); ben, 1660, 1828, 1830. — *2 pl. pr. ind.*, be, 1622, 1713, 1783. — *3 pl. pr. ind.*, ben, 932, 999, 1167, 1222, 1254, 1516, 1793, 1946; been, 1952; been, 1947 f, 1996 f (*both* : seen *inf.*); be 1894; be 1382 f (: she *pro.*); bee 752 f (: see *n.*); Arne set, 1008. — *2 sg. pr. subj.*, be, 1860; be, 1593 f (: the *pro.*). — *3 sg. pr. subj.*, be, 44, 276, 352, 408, 526, 722, 778, 802, 821, 838, 876, 1059, 1078, 1676, 1820, 1853, 2020; be, 927 f (: se *inf.*), 1081 f (: she *pro.*); bee, 803 f (: y-see *inf.*). — *1 pl. pr. subj.*, be, 673, 2107; ben, 1614. — *3 pl. pr. subj.*, be, 645, 1666. — *2 sg. impv.*, be, 519, 557, 581, 1405. — *2 pl. impv.*, be, 1978. — *1 sg. pt. ind.*, was, 59, 113, 129, etc.; was, 119 f (: glas *n.*), etc. — *3 sg. pt. ind.*, was, 82, 105, 112, 118, 130, 139, etc.; was, 141 f (: bras *n.*), 158 f (: allas *intj.*), 218 f (: Eneas *pr. n.*), etc.; nas, 486, 915, 1346, 1367, 1922, 1978, 2037; nas, 1296 f, 1358 f, 2068 f (: *all* : was *3 sg. pt. ind.*). — For the *plur. pret. ind.*, see § 109. — For the *pret. subj.*, see §§ 113, 114. — *Pp.*, be, *410; y-be, 1733 f (: we *pro.*); I-ben, 1138; y-been, 1338 f (: seen *inf.*).

wol, nyl. — *1 sg. pr. ind.*, wol, 65, 67, 143, 289, 601, 764, 782, 1086, 1113, 2098; wil, 772, 1057, 1427, 1864, 1880, 1913; will, 1068; wyl, 1884; will(e), 725 f (: skille *n.*); nyl, 56, 1255, 1329, 1822, 1856. — *2 sg. pr. ind.*, wolt, 631, 671,

1069 ; wilt, 993, 1080, 1102, 2099 ; of these the last two examples are in subjunctive constructions. —*3 sg. pr. ind.*, wol, 247, 359, 586, 662, 670, 790, *794, 2008, 2020; will, 1044. — *1 pl. pr. ind.*, wil, 886, 2102. — *2 pl. pr. ind.*, wol ye, 320. — *1 sg. pt.*, woldë hyt, **382**; wolde fayn, 1848 ; wolde her, **1505.** —*3 sg. pt.*, wolde lede, 942 ; wold[e] no, 1785 ; wolde haue, 302, 305, 1784 ; wolde envien, 1231 ; wolde he, 2073 ; wolde hir, 296. — *2 pl. pt.*, wolde, 1779 f (: nolde *2 pl. pt.*) ; nolde, 1780 f (: wolde *2 pl. pt.*). —*3 pl. pt.*, wolden honour, 1793 ; wolde they, 1712. — A few preterites manifestly subjunctive are indicated by Gothic figures ; in the main no distinction is tried for.

do. — *Infinitive*, see § 119, XIII. — *1 sg. pr. ind.*, do, 1024 f (: lo *intj.*). — *2 sg. pr. ind.*, doost, *1883. —*3 sg. pr. ind.*, dooth, 610, 1653, 1933 ; doth, 1036, 1042 ; dothe Apparence, 265 ; dothe amys, 269 ; dothe where, 1648 ; dothe the, 2116 ; doth(e), 2052 f (: sothe *pred. adj. sg.*). —*3 pl. pr. ind.*, don, 1522 ; doon, 1267, 2154. — *1 sg. pr. subj.*, do, 1099, 1788. — *2 sg. impv.*, doon, 1859. — *1 sg. pt. ind.*, did al, 2132.— *2 sg. pt. ind.*, didęst, 1846. —*3 sg. pt. ind.*, did he, 1688 ; did hem, 474 ; did hym, 259 ; did this, 1636. — *Pp.*, do, 354, 361 ; doo, 372 f (: thertoo), 395 ; don, 1630, 1694, 1732 ; doon 1698, 1737 ; doon, 1775 f (: euerychon) ; y-doon, 1812.

go. — *Infinitive*, see § 119, XIII. — *2 sg. pr. ind.*, goost, 655. — *3 sg. pr. ind.*, gooth, 806. — *1 sg. pr. subj.*, goo, 1055. — *3 sg. pr. subj.*, goo, 1674 f (: soo *adv.*). —*3 pl. pr. subj.*, goon, 1768. — *2 sg. impv.*, goo, 317, 1790. — *2 pl. impv.*, goo, 1561, 1622. — For *present participle*, see § 120. — *Pp.*, goo, 434 ; y-goo, 802 f (: euer moo) ; for-goo, 115 f (: two *num.*) ; goon, 1110 f (: anoon *adv.*) ; (a)goon, 365 f (: anoon *adv.*).

haue. — *Infinitive*, hauę be, 410 ; hauę take, 424 ; hauę tolde, 996 ; hauę truly, 1045 ; hauę wonder, 1069 ; hauę name, 1312 ; hauę no, 1695 ; hauę my, 1716 ; hauę that, 1855 ; haue, 577, 1617, 1619, 1715, 1794 ; han, 958, 1610, 1667, 1735, 1795, 1815, 1848, 1872, 1929, 2104. — *1 sg. pr. ind.*, hauę yow, 109, 529 ; hauę do, 354 ; hauę the, 606 ; hauę be-fore, 839 ; hauę seyde, 883 ; hauę yit, 1182, etc. ; haue, 814, 823, 854, etc. ; hauę herd, 1059 ; hauę herde, 1931. — *2 sg. pr. ind.*, hast, 200, 616, 620, 644, 653, etc. ; haste a, 607. —*3 sg. pr. ind.*, hath, 49, 100, 358, 377, 384, 612, 614, etc. — *1 pl. pr. ind.*, han, 1054, 1613, 1694, 1698, 1732, 1831. — *2 pl. pr. ind.*, hauę ye, 330, 1716. — *3 pl. pr. ind.*, han, 1168, 1225, 1630, 1632, 1737, 1766, 1832, 1852, 1854,

1899, 2056; hau*e* hys, 626. — *1 sg. pr. subj.*, hau*e* I, 1471.
— *2 sg. pr. subj.*, hau*e* hem, 1009. —*3 sg. pr. subj.*, hau*e* my, 1877. — *1 pl. pr. subj.*, hau*e* yow, 339; han, 1762. — *2 pl. pr. subj.*, hau*e* in, 823; hau*e* deserued, 1621. — *3 pl. pr. subj.*, hau*e* the, 41. — For the *imperative*, see §§ 115, III., 118. — For the *preterite indicative*, see §§ 102, 106. — For the *preterite subjunctive*, see § 113. — For the *perfect participle*, see § 121, IV.

LIFE.

I WAS born in Charlotte County, Virginia, December 12, 1867, and had my early academic training in the private and public schools of my native township. After one year at the then Virginia Agricultural and Mechanical College, I enlisted at the Virginia Military Institute in 1885 and four years later was graduated with the B. S. degree. The year following my graduation I was assistant professor of Modern Languages and Tactics in my *alma mater*, and the next three years was commandant of cadets in Wentworth Military Academy, Lexington, Missouri. In 1893 I entered the University of Virginia, where for two years I pursued graduate courses in Latin and English Language under Professors Peters and Garnett. The session of 1895–6 found me again in service at the Virginia Military Institute, and the two succeeding years were passed at St. Albans School, Radford, Virginia, as master of Latin and French. I returned to the University of Virginia the current session for further prosecution of my graduate studies, and hold, by award of the Visitors of the University, the John Y. Mason fellowship.

Grateful acknowledgment for their instruction and kindly interest is made the several professors who have directed my studies. To Professor Harrison, under whom the present paper has been brought to completion, my special thanks are due, as well for encouragement and guidance as for the loan of many serviceable books from his private library.